ADVANCE PRAISE

Becc's 30+ years of experience and wisdom is evident inside *Cut the Shit.* Her expertise in healing and transformation helped her create a highly valuable and practical guide that anyone can use to enhance their life. She addresses real life problems that we all go through, and gives the reader an opportunity to transform."

–**Tony Mitchell**, Life Coach for Empaths

Becc Nelson has created the perfect life guidebook, blending both real-life stories and fourteen rules that will completely reframe your thinking. Pick up this book if you're ready to shift your mindset and transform your life, receiving insights from an author that is an absolute expert in her field.

– **Lindsay Marino**, International Psychic Medium & Mentor

A bitch slap in my face, but in a good way!

(And if Becc Nelson writes a sequel, I'll be the first to turn the other cheek.)

Good teachers empower through their knowledge. Great teachers empower through their observations. The wisdom in Becc Nelson's book draw deeply from the well of her observation and as such it gifts readers with a road map for a more liberated, happier journey through life. Becc calls that road map "The Rules." These are a set of clear and simple principles that each one of us can practice in the real world nitty gritty mess that we call relationships, work, health and money.

Follow this book's guidance and you will not only be more liberated and more authentically loving, you'll also impart the same experience to those you love as well as those you struggle to love.

–Tom Poland, Chief Leadsologist

REFRAME YOUR THINKING, REGAIN YOUR LIFE

BECC NELSON, MS, LMFT

CUT THE SHIT

ISBN: 978-0-578-37746-9

Cover and Interior Design by
Transcendent Publishing

TRANSCENDENT
publishing

The content of this book is for informational purposes only and is not intended to diagnose, treat, cure, or prevent any condition or disease. You understand that this book is not intended as a substitute for consultation with a licensed practitioner. The use of this book implies your acceptance of this disclaimer.

Printed in the United States of America.

Dedication

To my mom, my husband, my brother and my daughter –
the four people in my life who love me unconditionally
and believe in me always.

CONTENTS

Foreword

by Sunny Dawn Johnston

Cut the Shit! I LOVE the title of this book. I think it's perfect! I know not everyone relates to this, but for some of us, the *gentle* approach to help and healing doesn't work. There is a time and place for the loving, soft, gentle energy and support of a best friend, for sure. As a spiritual guide and mentor for over two decades, I have seen many clients that thrive with that type of guidance and support. It is important. But, that isn't for everyone. If you are anything like me, you are someone that sometimes (not as often now that I have fifty years of life under my belt) needs to hear it a little louder, a little stronger—more like the spiritual 2x4—so you don't miss it. It helps to know which type of learner you are. I always desire to be the "grace and ease" learner, and have discovered that sometimes, I just need it more in my face.

Healing, I believe, comes down to personal responsibility. Some people don't want it; they want to play the blame game. Yet, some thrive on it. Bottom line is that either way, we have to take personal responsibility for our lives and what we are creating in them. That certainly doesn't mean that everything "bad" that has happened in your life is your fault, and yet, it does mean that it *is* your responsibility to heal it. No one is going to step up and do your healing for you. They can't. It's yours to heal. It's up to you and those that you invite into your support team.

Cut the Shit helps you to recognize that it is time for you to take your power back from those you have given it to (or who you feel have taken it) and get to work on owning your own healing. It is the type of book that people like me need. One that just tells it like it is and doesn't sugarcoat it. Becc has done a beautiful job weaving in activities and stories to help you see different perspectives. As you read through the book, you will see ways that you can call yourself out on your excuses or limited mindset, and make the changes you desire to live the best life you have ever dreamed of.

Now, I know for me, when I saw that there were a bunch of rules in the book, I had a little cringe at first; maybe you did too. Rules have never been my favorite thing. But, these rules are more like guideposts along the way—reminders that if you are taking particular actions, it is likely taking you off course from your desired outcome. The rules are truly beautiful mile markers along this journey we call life to keep us present, open, and aware of the story we might be telling ourselves ... and the rules give us the guidance to tell a *new* story. One of hope, possibility, and choice.

If you are ready to change your mind, own your "stuff" and heal your life, then this book is a great start to that journey. You have the right book, at the perfect time: right now. Enjoy the journey ... I sure did.

–**Sunny Dawn Johnston**, Psychic Medium and Spiritual Mentor; Author of *Invoking the Archangels* and *The Love Never Ends*

"To be aware of a single shortcoming within oneself is more useful than to be aware of a thousand in somebody else."

– **H. H. Tenzin Gyatso**, the XIV Dalai Lama of Tibet

Introduction

I GET YOU

"You serve your clients best when you work both with your knowledge and your wisdom."

These words, told to me by one of my mentors, really stuck. I had been working in the field of emotional healing as a licensed marriage and family therapist since 1992. I had also, during my years in service, counseled children, adults, and couples with mental health and substance abuse challenges. I was an expert in all things in transformation; I had a master's degree and all the "knowledge" necessary to do this work. What I had not factored in, as I began to incorporate spiritual healing into my practice, was the power of "wisdom." This – as my mentor so astutely pointed out – came from applying what I already knew to my own life situations to raise my vibration and accelerate the growth of my spirit and mind. It is from this place of wisdom and knowledge that I share the same lessons so you too can transform and develop for your highest and best good.

Do you feel like you have more problems than most other people? Do you wonder if you're "being punished" for something, or describe yourself as having a black cloud over your head?

I frequently ask my clients these questions during the first few sessions of the assessment process, and more often than not, the answer is yes. They feel no one understands them, that no one gets just how much they have endured. Just when they finally start to get their "heads above water," something happens to bring them back down again.

Is this you? Do you have low energy, struggle with sleep problems, struggle to feel any joy in your life, and struggle with trusting anyone? Have you lost hope that anyone can understand or help you, and feel you might just as well give up on hoping for anything other than a life of struggle and mediocrity?

Maybe you would not describe your life as all that bad. Perhaps you can't relate to everything I described in the previous paragraph. You have blessings in your life and can identify lots of things you are grateful for, and that's wonderful. Yet, you feel like there is something more for you. You have trouble "being in the moment," and also wonder what your purpose is in this life. If someone asks you what you enjoy doing you find yourself searchin' for an answer, except to say spending time with your family and friends. You feel almost guilty for thinking something is missing. After all, you have everything you need, and shouldn't that be enough? You "should" feel happy since everything seems good, yet you can't ignore that nagging feeling that something else is out there, just beyond your reach.

To the outside world, you appear to hold it all together. No one, except for maybe a very select few, has any idea that you're falling apart inside. No one knows that most of the time you function at a bare minimum; no one has a hint of the battle raging inside you, or that you are teetering at the edge of a cliff.

Then one thing happens and you can't deal with it as well as you once could; it becomes harder to hide your struggle from others. You fall off the cliff and continue to do so, each time finding it harder to get back up. By the time you call for help you've run out of hope that things can be different. Maybe you are at the point where you have given up asking, because when you cried out in the past no one answered the call. You become more resentful, angry, and withdrawn.

You consider yourself a spiritual person and feel you ought to do good deeds in the world, thus you attempt to deal with your emotional struggles and bad days by helping others and taking the high road. Yet, you find this isn't working, and when you need to tap into that pool for yourself the rewards are meager. Finally, you realize that putting the needs of others before your own is only leaving you disillusioned and feeling powerless.

You read things about "helper burnout," which tell you to prioritize yourself and your own needs and stop allowing others to sap your energy. Your solution is to do just that. You have been too passive, you tell yourself, and now you need to shut out those you identify as having been taking advantage of you. These are the people in your immediate circle – partners, parents, best friends, kids, or coworkers – who will be most impacted by your new thought process. You will now take back the power you have given away freely for so long, and you decide the best way to do this is to become aggressive. After all, being passive has always led to you not asking for what you needed, or those needs going unheard and not honored. Being passive meant you allowed others to say and do things you experienced as disrespectful and belittling. Others, you felt, were putting you down or not understanding how things may have impacted you, and now you're going to educate them on how inaccurate they were.

You decide that you will not give anyone permission to put you last or down ever again. Perhaps friends or even therapists have told you that your anger allows you to regain your power and will help you feel confident and alive again. Maybe you were advised to stay angry in order to stay "empowered." What you don't realize, however, is that this advice is perpetuating your victimhood, reinforcing the thoughts that no one understands you or how difficult life has been for you. At the same time, you put yourself in the position of authority, not only to stick up for yourself but to take inventory of others' lives and even tell them what it is they need to do to live the "right way." Some may argue with you about this, but you tell yourself your intentions are pure and justified so you have every right to tell them exactly what you think of their situation and how they need to change. If others don't like it then "too bad."

While it may initially feel better than being passive, maintaining this level of energy, protection, and anger is exhausting! Emotions have an important role in assisting us with self-protection and preservation. Emotions such as anger, anxiety, and fear can help us intuitively stay away from situations that are not healthy. However, as with everything in life, these emotions need to be kept in balance. They serve a purpose in a "fight or flight" situation, meaning they can be useful and protective in an emergency situation, but if these emotions are allowed to persist past the point of responding to that situation, they can have a paradoxical impact on the body, mind, and soul. Over time they can create issues and problems that may be permanent and even deadly. This brings about a self-fulfilling prophecy: the negative impressions and thoughts you allowed yourself to manifest about the world, and your place in it, are supported.

Once you become critical of others and aggressive in an attempt to stand up for yourself, your vibrations and affect (your observable emotional response) change. You have already told yourself no one cares about you and that you are all alone; now you adopt the "posture" that you can't count on anyone but yourself. You may see yourself as a "realist," but you have actually become very negative. Others keep their distance because it's draining for them to be around you, which further reinforces your belief that you can't count on anyone. Your body begins to give you signals that your changes are not supporting your true and best self. These signals may come in the form of headaches, muscle aches, difficulties sleeping, and irritability. The more you ignore these signs and symptoms, the more they persist and even get louder.

Maybe, in your loneliness and self-destructiveness, you also engage in other poor habits, such as drinking alcohol or using other substances (illicit and/or prescribed). Perhaps you seek validation through sex, spending money, or overeating. The gains from these changes you've made are meager, but you continue living this way because you feel better "sticking up" for yourself than just standing around and letting everyone take advantage of you. And, while you may not realize it, telling everyone what they need to do differently is easier than looking deeper into yourself.

Essentially, what you had intended to be your "solution" has only created more problems. On some level you understand this, and may even have sought out healing experiences, only to find the people you worked with were "nice" but not effective.

Is this where you are?

For the most part, people who get to this place tell me they have tried "everything." The healers they've worked with empathized with their story and agreed they did the right thing by creating better boundaries for themselves. The problem is, many therapists teach their clients to create these boundaries but do not teach them how to do so with balance. Balance comes when you learn to stand up for yourself in a way that is not aggressive or passive, but assertive. This is the best of both worlds, allowing you to stand up for yourself without having to put others down, lower your vibrations or drain your own energy.

In this book I will share with you the ways in which people, including me and many of my clients, sabotage themselves, usually without their awareness. I will then share "The Rules," passed to me by my guides, that assisted me in my own growth and healing. When you get to this section, read each rule, allowing yourself space to think about each one and how you may relate to it. I won't lie: admitting to yourself that you have broken many, if not all of them, isn't "pretty." You may even feel defensive and angry. However, if you are honest with yourself and stick with the process of working with them, you will experience and receive healing. I can tell you this because I have gone through and faced each one of them, and the result has been incredibly powerful growth and the stronger connection to self that I was meant to express. My wish is that you allow and receive this guidance for yourself, and that you challenge yourself to grow in ways you struggled to do in the past. I promise you are worth the effort.

PART I

Reframe Your Thinking

Chapter One

MY STORY

In March of 2020, I began going through a spiritual "awakening" – you know, the kind you may have read about in various books. Like most people, my life until that point had had many hills and valleys, though I often felt as if I'd had more valleys than hills. I'm not currently in a place where I can get into too much detail about my childhood, however, I will say that I experienced many adversities. I was an awkward kid who talked too much and felt socially disconnected. I also probably had undiagnosed learning disabilities that seriously impacted my education and, worse yet, my self-esteem and confidence – issues that were compounded by other factors in my environment. I was a fighter, though, and refused to let these obstacles become an excuse to not live my best life. I worked hard, and I had many blessings. Yet despite my tireless efforts to emulate those who seemed to have a more fulfilling existence, I always felt as if something was missing.

I met my husband Ed when I was in my early twenties and we have been together for over thirty years. He is my best friend and we have a good life together, however, like any married couple, we've been through many ups and downs and had our share of struggles. Finances were often an issue, and it seemed that whenever we did manage to squirrel away some money something would inevitably happen to drain our savings. Also,

I would have loved to be able to work part-time and spend the bulk of my days at home with our daughter, but that simply wasn't possible. On the other hand, the bills always got paid, and I couldn't really complain. Things were just "okay."

I had been working in the healing field since 1992 when Ed began talking about starting our own practice. We are both very ambitious, creative, and driven people and had plenty of ideas about how to establish and grow a thriving business. Yet initially I was hesitant to move forward. Seeing my own clients was fine, but I was worried that dealing with mounting insurance regulations and personnel issues involved with running a larger practice would become overwhelming. But Ed can be very convincing, and Hope Counseling & Mediation Center INC opened in January of 2011.

My journey as a mother has also been an interesting one, filled with twists and turns, joys and often seemingly insurmountable challenges. I had always wanted children and was overjoyed when I gave birth to Taylor eighteen months into our marriage. You know that phrase, "When they made her they broke the mold"? Well, Taylor was the most independent and defiant child I had ever encountered. I remember having my first "parent-teacher meeting" at her preschool when she was two, and all they wanted to talk about was how she didn't want to follow the rules. Each year I thought things would get better and that I would feel comfortable having another child. That never happened; in fact, things only got worse. I still count my daughter's high school years among the most trying and difficult of my life, and I consider it a miracle that we emerged from them as a family unit. When she graduated, I was sure things would get easier. There was no way I could have known we were on the precipice of a much deeper valley.

Shortly thereafter, Ed lost his job of eighteen years when the company moved that position to another state. This event threw us – individually and as a family – into a very dark time. We were not prepared for how much the job market and the business world had changed since he had last looked for work, or how he would struggle just to get anyone to respond to his applications. It got to be so disheartening that Ed eventually decided he wanted to work instead for our family healing center. I knew this was not the right time for him to do so, but despite my objections he stopped actively looking for work and joined our business part-time. Sure enough, the business was soon struggling under the weight of the additional paycheck and health insurance costs.

Ed then decided we needed to let go of my mother, who had been working for us, so he could take over the office manager position full-time. I already knew this was not a position he would enjoy or derive any satisfaction from. In addition, I was also unable to bring on new therapists (we had recently lost a few) for the first time since we had opened. I had maxed-out a business line of credit as well as the overdraft account, and I feared we may have no choice but to close our doors. We both knew it wasn't working and it was putting a terrible strain on the business and our marriage, yet, he stayed – an attempt to avoid the stress of resuming his job search. In the end, we wound up having to lay him off and I was left with thousands in debt and unable to bring on any new therapists for about two years.

Taylor started working for the business but had no car of her own, so I couldn't leave for work every day until she was ready. Since she was in no hurry to get there I would get in hours later than I wanted to each day. Between dealing with Ed and Taylor's struggles to find happiness in their lives and the financial toll, I hit an all-time low. And, as if that wasn't enough, in March of 2020 the pandemic hit. I figured we would have to close for sure and I would end up at some job I completely hated just to pay the bills. During that time I'm pretty sure I cried just about every day.

How did I get to this place? I thought. *I'm a good person. I'm honest, hardworking, and I've never asked or expected anything from anyone. I feel like I treat people the way I want to be treated. Why can't good things really happen for me? Why do I always feel like I have to struggle to just get by?*

Truly, I felt like I was being punished for something. That maybe in a past life I was not a good person and I was paying for it in this lifetime. I prayed and asked for help, but nothing changed.

Have you ever said these things to yourself?

I had a talk with my friend Debbie, who is also a medium. I told her how difficult things had become over the previous few years and she knew I was at a breaking point. Debbie gave me advice I cherished and began using that very day. She told me to start acting as if I already had what I wanted and tell my angels and God just how much I appreciated it. I know now this is the basic premise of manifesting what you want in your life.

From that day I said a prayer of gratitude for the "abundance of resources" I had – therapists, finances, and vendors that bless me and that I would bless, and so on. Within a few months we received grants from the government to help us through the pandemic. LinkedIn allowed me to run an ad for a new therapist for free because we are considered healthcare and by the middle of that summer we had brought one on board. By the end of the summer we were also joined by a friend who was a licensed therapist and had been saying for years that she wanted to join the practice. I had an uncle who passed away and my aunt offered me his low-mileage vehicle, which we were able to get on the road by the fall for my daughter to drive. As if by some miracle the shift I had made in my attitude and daily thoughts slowly allowed a manifestation of abundance.

There was one more piece I needed to be in place in order to shift my energies for my highest and best good. One of the things I prayed for when I was in my darkest space was a mentor. At the time I hadn't been connecting with the spiritual world, let alone the notion that I was a psychic/medium. However, as my energy began to shift it became clear that I was being led to experiences, courses, and people involved in the metaphysical arts.

One of these early experiences involved my father's brother, Danny, who had passed from cancer back in 1987, when I was sixteen. Uncle Danny was a marine, earning three purple hearts during his service in Vietnam, and spent his last days in a VA hospital. Looking back, I realize that he had suffered from severe PTSD and struggled with adjusting to regular everyday life. Despite his emotional issues, he and I were very close. He was affectionate, loving, and fiercely protective of me. I was devastated by his loss, and had no way of knowing how integral he would be in helping me discover my gifts.

Uncle Danny began letting his presence be known in very subtle ways. Objects I knew for certain I had put in a specific spot would be moved to an entirely different place. Someone in the family would mention his name, or a picture of him would pop up out of the blue. I would sense the smell of pipe smoke, reminding me of the pipe he smoked. (That pipe still sits on the shelf in my living room!). Then, during one of my couple's counseling sessions, he stopped being so subtle.

The husband suddenly started talking about being in the Marines and his active time in Vietnam, then a particular man he'd served with who he described as "funny and crazy." This man often spoke about his mother and would even read her letters to their unit. The more he talked, the more I realized he was talking about Uncle Danny! Sure enough, he said my uncle's name, and I could swear I felt his presence in the room. He was letting me know he was around and supporting me, and even bringing in clients he knew I could help. Though I was amazed by the experience, I didn't make the connection to say, "I am a medium." I now realize this was partly because I was in denial and fearful of what would happen if I allowed things to open up.

In October of 2018, Danny became bolder still. Ed and I had just returned from a vacation in Puerto Rico, where we celebrated our twenty-fifth anniversary. I was about to go shopping to restock the house when I got a text from Ed, who had gone into our detached garage to do some chores. It was a picture of a huge, overstuffed chair from our office that had broken a few years earlier. He had left it in the corner of the garage to fix, and it had been buried there ever since. Now, there it was, right behind the garage door, and Ed was asking if I knew how it had gotten there. I replied "nope," erased the picture, and went to the store.

While I was there, a woman stopped me and said, "Excuse me. I don't know if you believe in this stuff or not, but there is a man standing next to you jumping up and down and yelling, and he is mad! He says he doesn't know what he has to do to show you he is around." She went on to describe my Uncle Danny in exact detail, then repeated everything he'd told her, outlining how he moved the chair and that my husband had texted me the picture. He told her he needed me to understand that he was around and to pay attention to him. I listened in shocked silence as the woman relayed messages he had for me and my father, then walked away. I don't remember finishing my shopping, but from that day on I began spending more time being aware of both Danny's presence and the presence of Spirit in general.

By October of 2020 I had been blessed to find a tribe of people who provided the support I needed to grow, as well as that mentor I had been praying for. She had been a licensed therapist just like me and had chosen to move into spiritual coaching. One of our sessions in particular was so powerful I knew I would never forget it.

For years, people had sought me out for healing and guidance, both personally and professionally. I know now that I am empathic, and so they were naturally drawn to my energy. But though I provided guidance and energy to others, I had not been able to bring blessings into my own life. In addition, some – including my own family – who came to me for counseling did not offer to do the same when I reached out for help. I remember wondering if I had been put on this planet simply to serve others, never getting what I wanted. As I mentioned early, I felt things were "okay" but never "great" and, in my mind, I had a lot of "evidence" to support the notion that I was not meant to experience true happiness in my life.

I posed the question to my spiritual mentor: Did God indeed put some people on the planet solely to serve others, with no expectation of abundant blessings for themselves? At this point I was not feeling sorry for myself. I wasn't saying "poor me." I was simply trying to understand my reality so I could reduce my expectations and manage disappointments. I was preparing myself for confirmation of my hypothesis so I could adjust my personal goals.

First, I learned that God certainly does *not* decide that certain people are here to do unto others without reciprocity and abundance. Just as – if not more – importantly, I learned that by putting this false notion out to the spiritual realm, I was actually manifesting it as my destiny. Whenever I told Spirit, "I must be here for the purpose of serving others while not expecting blessings back in return," the Universe was giving me that experience. It was helping me fulfill my stated purpose by sending me people who need to be healed. The Universe also "supported" me whenever I thought or said that no one reciprocated the energy I put into relationships, by bringing me people who did not reciprocate my energy. Apparently, all this time the angelic realm had simply delivered what I had told them to!

Armed with this knowledge, I began to put out into the Universe exactly what and who I wanted in my world each day. I began to use this universal law of attraction to my benefit right away to attract blessings and abundance into my life.

Moreover, I became keenly aware that some of the interventions I had been using with my clients were actually divinely inspired and intuitively created. "The Rules," which became the basis of this book, are based on those guiding principles. I recall sitting down to write them out formally for the first time and feeling the energy of them once they were all together in a concrete form. Within a few days, I read them to a mentor, further fueling their energies. She responded with silence at first, then said, "I need to follow a few of these at my house!" The Rules now had their own identity, and they came out in divine timing just as I was preparing to write my first book.

The Rules had been provided to me because as a mental health therapist, healer, and psychic medium, I am in a unique position to be an agent of change for others. First, however, I needed to go through the process of learning to manage my own energy and understand how to work with manifesting to heal myself. I had to experience this transformation myself in order to help others transform.

Like me, you may already feel as if you are doing everything you can to bring good things into your life. You may try to understand why bad things keep happening, why you are doing all you can to be good to others but don't feel good things come to you. I understand all too well the possible pitfalls you can encounter in the process of change.

It has been my experience that one's intended solutions to their problem tend to create more problems and attract exactly the opposite of what you really want. Since applying The Rules to my own life on a daily basis, this no longer happens. These rules assist me in managing my energy and raising my own vibration in every interaction with others.

Each rule is its own chapter, which includes examples from my years as a therapist and encourages you to identify how they may have impacted you in your own life. When you learn to manage your own vibrations and energy, you too will be in a position to work with the dysfunctional patterns of thought that have likely contributed to a history of unsatisfying relationships throughout your lifetime. While The Rules are not for everyone; they will, however, benefit anyone who realizes that what they thought were solutions may actually be negatively impacting their ability to create positive and sustainable change. They likely identify as self-sufficient, spiritual, and responsible. They are also willing to identify their insecurities and negative self-talk that has kept them from achieving their goals. Finally, they must be willing to take an honest look at themselves and hear constructive suggestions.

As "The Rules" took shape and became a living document, I invited a few friends to read through them and provide feedback. I found myself becoming so excited when people talked about the examples from each rule and related them to their own memories. I felt so blessed and honored when they told me these learnings left them feeling more enlightened and on a path to personal growth. This helped me to see that my book could benefit anyone who wishes to improve themselves and receive blessings in their life. All they must do is be open and allow themselves to be guided through the process, just as I was.

Chapter Two

SURRENDER TO
THE PROCESS

It was back in graduate school when I first heard that people usually come for help when their intended solutions create bigger problems. This profound statement stuck with me, and over my twenty-five-plus years as a marriage and family therapist and expert in transformation, I have seen evidence of it countless times. Indeed, it was one of two common obstacles to making the changes necessary to achieve a more satisfying life. The other is a history of unsatisfying relationships that tend to play out in many areas of their lives.

Most everyone can identify at least one unsatisfying relationship in their lifetime; however, if this is a pattern that has repeated itself in relationships with your romantic partners, one or both parents, siblings, friends, bosses and coworkers, jobs, food, money, or yourself, then it's likely been wreaking havoc in your life. For although the nature of these relationships may vary, I have found they tend to share one thing in common: they are causing the person physical and/or emotional pain, despite their best efforts to be good and morally ethical.

Another common thing I hear is that the person feels they are "being punished" for something. As was the case with me, they don't understand their torment is not coming from God or some other outside force, but their own energy and where they are placing it. Does this speak to you? Can you see how the energy you are putting into having more satisfying relationships is destroying you from the inside out? Your emotions are negative, toxic, destructive, overwhelming, dangerous, tiring, draining, exhausting, and low-vibrational; they bring you away from your best self. You don't want to be here, but you can't help it. Despite all your efforts to do the right thing, these patterns keep playing out. You begin to think that this is your lot in life, that you are not meant to be happy.

Think about what choices you have made over the years in an effort to change these patterns of unsatisfying relationships. Let's say, for example, that this relationship was with a co-worker. You might have tried to address the issue head-on, by having a conversation with the other person, or maybe you went to HR in an attempt to have someone understand your side of the story. You may have also done things that were not as direct, like talking about that person with other coworkers so they would side with you, validate you, and become allies.

These strategies, either conscious or unconscious, may have brought some relief but never provided any lasting results. In fact, they may have even created more tension and conflict, which for you results in feelings of hopelessness and being out of control. You might experience anger, resentment, frustration, irritability, anxiety, depression, loneliness, and perhaps even exhaustion and other physical symptoms that only serve to keep you stuck in an endless, unhealthy loop.

At some point you may have told yourself that the only way to climb out of the hole you keep falling (or being thrown) into is to come back swinging. If you fight, you feel like you are getting back some of your control, as if fighting makes you more powerful, in charge and making progress. You tell yourself you aren't taking these blows "lying down," that you won't allow anyone to ever hurt you or put you down again. No one, including yourself, will ever see you as weak or a pushover ever again. You will never allow yourself to be lied to, betrayed, forsaken, cheated on, or belittled by anyone. After all, this isn't your problem; it's everyone else's.

In your effort to stand up for yourself, however, you can cause much bigger problems. Why? Because the person or situation you are making the object of your wrath is not the true source of the problem. That person or people have likely left your life some time ago – they may even be dead – and those painful situations may have taken place long ago, perhaps in childhood. Another possibility is that they are still part of your immediate tribe and you risk losing them if you confront them directly.

Instead, you project anger towards others in your life who are triggering that original wound. You make yourself the aggressor and let the other person see that you are in the "one-up" position. Perhaps you yell, become demanding, use "should" statements. Maybe you tell the other person consistently how disappointed and angry you are, leaving them feeling inadequate – essentially, you are recreating cycles of inter-actions that hurt you. In this process, you may tell yourself you have defeated the enemy. You have advanced your own level by putting the "bad man" in their place. You have shown the world you will no longer be the victim.

You know what happens? The feeling of achievement you tell yourself you are entitled to never happens. You continue to feel "less than," and your body begins to feel the effects of the constant "flight or fight" cycle, leaving you exhausted – emotionally, physically, mentally, and spiritually. You feel hopeless, isolated from your support system, and over-whelmed.

You may tell yourself it's better to be alone anyway, because then no one can hurt you. You can't feel vulnerable if you don't see anyone, right? Your spiritual health takes a serious hit. You struggle to hear your own intuition because your vibrations are so low, and your best solutions and efforts only led to more problems. How could you ever recover and trust again?

In the process of trying to find your power, you have used all your energy on investments that pay low or no dividends. When you are angry, irritable, accusatory, yelling, and ag-gressive, you are hoping to be seen, heard, and understood. Instead, you are seen as out of control, angry, and controlling; you may even be called, "crazy." You are also drained and completely overwhelmed.

This is where The Rules come in. The Rules require us to allow for trust and surrender. When someone first hears this their first reaction is often silence, yet I can almost hear their thoughts: "Becc, you don't understand... If I don't fight back,

I will be vulnerable. If I don't tell others what I want and fight for myself, no one will hear me. No one will know just how much I'm hurting. No one else will fight for me. People will get away with hurting me…no one will be held accountable. No one will learn their lesson. I will remain in the 'one down' position. I will be stuck here and no one will ever see me. I'll be stuck here forever."

There is another way. It requires faith in the healer, submission to the fact that your best solution ultimately became the problem. Your vibrations are low and your resources are spent. It is difficult to have anyone understand how letting go can save them. Total submission to The Rules allows one to be heard, but in a way that leaves you feeling less exhausted. You find you can allow yourself to be on level ground without having to put anyone else "one down" and/or putting yourself on a pedestal. It requires complete faith and trust in the care provider and feels like you're looking straight down to the bottom of a cliff. I get it. I've been there. But if you believe and have faith, it works.

Unless you fully commit, I can't explain it to you. You have to allow and receive. It's as simple, and as scary, as that.

Exercise in Reflection and Preparation for Surrender

Take a moment here to reflect on what has come up for you so far, then answer the following questions:

Upon reflecting on my life, how do I identify with the notion that I have a history of unsatisfying relationships?

_____

_____

_____

_____

_____

_____

_____

What are some of the feelings I experience as I read through this chapter and reflect on what changes I may need to make?

_____

_____

_____

_____

_____

_____

_____

Reflect on this question: What do I fear may happen if I begin to make changes? (For example, If I stop being so angry maybe I will feel vulnerable.)

_____

_____

_____

_____

_____

_____

_____

_____

_____

_____

_____

_____

_____

_____

_____

_____

_____

_____

_____

_____

_____

Chapter Three

WHEN YOUR SOLUTION IS THE PROBLEM

Throughout this book I've been discussing how the "solutions" people create often worsen their problems and/or create new ones. This is so common that I ask clients in the first session what they see as the "problem" and what they have already done to attempt to resolve their problem. This allows me to create a treatment plan and form goals and related objectives using new strategies, rather than wasting time on measures that have not been productive. Healers who do not properly assess what has already been attempted run the risk of unknowingly enabling current unhealthy and dysfunctional patterns. Additionally, this assessment gives me an opportunity to see where unsuccessful solutions contributed to and created other issues.

In some instances, someone's attempted solutions can lead to behaviors that are maladaptive. The person is really seeking to minimize their symptoms and existing triggers; however, in doing so they take the path of least resistance, the quick fix. People also tend to turn to solutions that have worked for them in the past but may not work in the current situation. For example, the solutions that may have worked when they were single are not appropriate for their romantic relationship or the family.

For example, someone with a history of mild to moderate depression may come home each day from work and have a few glasses of wine or beer. They have figured out that drinking a few drinks each night helps them "wind-down" and "relax" after a stressful day. They may say it also assists in calming their brain down at night so they can sleep straight through. In their mind this is a reasonable solution to managing symptoms of depression because they can still go to work each day, they don't drink and drive, and they can get through the week without having to take any medications.

Yes, this behavior may make you feel better in the moment; after all, alcohol shifts you into an altered cognitive state, providing temporary relief of persistent unpleasant thoughts. However, drinking, particularly drinking to the point of intoxication, can lead to a host of other problematic situations and behaviors impacting their quality of life and creating more chaos. In this example, drinking is being used to self-medicate and manage depressive thoughts, but it actually exacerbates depression because it is a central nervous system depressant.

Clearly, if a client reports issues related to depression but not alcohol abuse, they feel a benefit from continuing their "solution." Unless there have been consequences related to drinking, attempts to address drinking patterns will likely meet resistance. Furthermore, taking away the coping mechanism of drinking to manage depression issues results in having to deal with depression head-on, which people want to avoid.

Another factor to consider is the effect their drinking has on their relationships. For example, though they do not drive drunk and still function each day, their partner may not agree their alcohol intake isn't problematic. Lisa had a few glasses of wine each night when she came home from work, saying she had "earned it" and needed to "wind-down" from a busy and stressful day. At first, Lisa occasionally would have a beer with dinner, but as her drinking increased over time, her husband began to complain. He said he would tell her things and the next day she wouldn't have any recollection of the conversation. Also, because Lisa often went to bed early after having a few glasses of wine, they were struggling to find time to connect during the week. In her mind, drinking was effective in "managing" her stressors. What she didn't realize or want to face was that it was also damaging her relationship.

People tend to become very attached to their attempted solution. They want the healer to assist them in making it "work," and any suggestions that they stop using it can result in an emotional conflict. An example of this is someone who self-medicates their anxiety by eating sugar, which makes them gain weight and negatively impacts several areas of their life. Clearly they enjoy the sugar, and though they know it's a problem they would love to find anything else they can change in order to avoid giving it up.

Cheating, which is something I see often when I work with couples, is another example of an attempted solution to underlying problems. A spouse can stray because of dissatisfaction with the marriage; however, infidelity can also be an indicator of other, personal issues that have nothing to do with the quality of the relationship. Whatever the case, it always causes a whole host of other problems to crop up.

For example, it is very common for the spouse who has been cheated on to struggle with trust and confidence issues. In an attempt to manage the emotional consequence of these issues, they become super-vigilant – checking the cheating spouse's text messages and emails, listening to their phone calls, and demanding to know where they have been at all times. They come to therapy expecting the healer to agree they have every right to make these demands with expectations of complete compliance. Typically, these expectations may be reasonable for a bit right after the event, however, in the long run they only contribute to resentment, exacerbating issues in the marriage.

It is also not unusual for couples to stop coming to me when they realize I do not agree that they have carte blanche to punish their spouse. In this case, the wronged spouse has "delivered" the other for help, but what they really want is for the healer to support their notion that their spouse is a "piece of shit" and is deserving of whatever punishment they see fit.

Sometimes, one's solutions don't cause another pain but are nonetheless ineffective and perpetuate the problem. For example, Brian came to counseling because he was waking up in the middle of the night and struggling to go back to sleep. When I asked him what he had tried he told me he'd started working out after dinner instead of in the morning, getting up to drink warm milk and pulling up social media at night in the hopes he would make himself tired. Turns out these solutions only activated his brain, making it more difficult to get a full night of quality sleep.

Maria came to counseling at the suggestion of her friends because she had been struggling to manage her sadness associated with the loss of her mother. She reported she was spending less time doing things she enjoyed, including time with friends, because she felt guilty about being happy when her mother was gone. Whenever she found herself thinking about her mother, she tried to make herself stop, which didn't work and only left her feeling vulnerable and weak. In her search for a solution Maria had created other behaviors that got in the way of the very real and healthy grief process – for example, she stopped talking about her grief to her friends because she felt they were tired of hearing it. We created a plan that included permission to think about her mother each day for a designated time. We also redefined her reaching out to friends as a healthy use of her resources rather than a sign of weakness. Engaging in activities she enjoyed was also reframed as a way for her to honor her mother's legacy, as well as her own spiritual and mental health.

Though these clients have very different stories, the guidance offered has a common theme. When you are trying to find resolution for your issue, first look at what you have done on your own that you would identify as attempted solutions. Assessing these measures (whether they are conscious or un- conscious) allows for opportunities to understand why they have not worked so you can pivot and create new ways of doing things. Also, when you turn to someone for coaching and guidance, do not expect this person to assist you in making your already attempted solution work. Remember, the definition of insanity is continuing to do the same thing and expecting different results, so make changes that will set yourself up for success.

Activity: Have My Intended Solutions Only Created More Problems?

Try this for yourself. Take a piece of paper (or use the template on the following page) and at the top write down a problem you would like to work on. Under that, make a list of the things you have done to attempt to solve the issue. Next, using a Likert scale from 1-5 (low to high), rate how effective you think the solution was at helping to manage your problem *and* didn't create other problems. Include any solutions that may not have been conscious but looking back were coping strategies, such as "smoke a cigarette, and "getting drunk." Any attempted solution that you rated less than 3 is likely creating or contributing to other problems. Any solutions that you rated 3 or above, continue to use and evaluate for effectiveness. Also, try combining two solutions together to see if that improves their effectiveness. For example, lots of people enjoy music and taking a walk on the beach. You could try listening to music while walking on the beach.

Problem: _____

List of Solutions: (things you have tried)	Rate 1-5 (low to high)
_____	_____
_____	_____
_____	_____
_____	_____
_____	_____
_____	_____
_____	_____
_____	_____
_____	_____
_____	_____
_____	_____
_____	_____

Chapter Four

THE ENTITLEMENT
SOLUTION

One of the most common "solutions" I've seen people use to attempt to solve an issue is entitlement. Entitlement is the belief that one is inherently deserving of privileges or special treatment. It's also a justification for blaming others for one's problems and expecting them to change in order to improve things. Essentially, people using the "Entitlement Solution" give themselves permission to act, think and behave in ways in which they assert themselves as a victim. When someone engages in entitlement, they absolve themselves of any responsibility for self-reflection or action. This self-defense mechanism is called deflection.

As mentioned, I frequently hear clients say they have done "everything" they could to solve a particular issue while also claiming that those close to them have done "nothing" to make changes. As a result of this perception, they give themselves permission to sit back and wait for others to make the next move. "It's their turn now," they say, "The ball is in their court." In doing so, they evaluate, and dismiss as subpar, any actual efforts made by the other party. They are also ignoring their own role in or control of the situation, including any flaws in their attempts at change.

Another example of entitlement is when in response to a "wrong" (real or perceived) that has been perpetrated against you, you engage in behaviors that may not otherwise be justifiable. An example would be a person who has been cheated on giving themselves permission to look at their partner's texts or emails. As mentioned earlier, the wronged party believes they have every right to do so until either their trust has been earned back or the other person has been properly punished. The problem with this particular entitlement solution is it contributes to a power struggle in the relationship. As any imbalance of power in a partnership is unhealthy, attempts to move past infidelity by putting the offended partner "in charge" will be unsuccessful.

Another example is when someone tells themselves they've had a poor lot in life and therefore have every right to act in any way that allows them to feel more empowered, even if it's disrespectful to someone else. They also believe they're justified in expecting special treatment from others. One of my clients was the youngest of ten children, all of whom had been abused while growing up. As a result, she felt she had the right to expect her siblings and other family members to take care of her; when they didn't she would lay on the guilt, which led them to avoid her. So you see, attempting to resolve painful situations with entitlement only creates messes in your life that impact your spiritual, mental and physical health.

Activity: What Are You "Entitled" To?

Here is a space for you to be honest with yourself. Use it to reflect on times you have said (either to yourself or out loud), "I am entitled to this because...." This can come in many forms, for example: "I'm entitled to a drink because I've had a tough day"; "I have every right to spy on my partner because they have betrayed my trust"; "I should be able to have time without the kids because I let you have it." Keep in mind here that we are not focusing on whether or not you would allow yourself time alone (or whatever example applies to you). You may indeed need whatever it is you are focusing on in your example. What we are focusing on here is the lower vibrational energy associated with acting entitled to do, say, think or engage in anything. Allow yourself to reflect on this lower vibrational energy so you may reveal it, and heal it.

I'm entitled to this because...

_____

_____

_____

_____

_____

_____

_____

_____

_____

_____

_____

Chapter Five

REFRAMING

I have been a healer for thirty years and have worked with people who are ready for transitions but struggle with blocks that get in the way of their efforts. I have worked in emergency services and assessment, methadone maintenance, intensive outpatient, partial hospital, inpatient and residential levels of care in both substance abuse and mental health programs. I have also assisted, through mediation, divorcing couples transition from married life to co-parenting arrangements. Whether I am working with adolescents or adults, individuals or couples, I've found the most powerful tool by far, one that consistently allows clients to transition into higher vibrational levels for their highest and best good, is reframing.

The act of reframing is an active decision to perceive or express an event, words, concepts or plans differently. We receive information all day, every day through our senses, including our intuition. Our brains process and act on this information, influenced by many factors that can include past experiences, teachings from others and genetics, among other things. The problem is, we often do so unconsciously, with no awareness that it is actually a decision.

In truth, we are born with only two innate reactions: that of being startled by loud noises and an automatic reaction to falling. All the other reactions to stimuli are learned and formed by experiences and the other variables mentioned above. The good news is, this means we are able to make different choices and allow new behaviors and thoughts. That said, this can be a painful and difficult journey because we keep getting triggered by the factors that caused us to develop our reactions in the first place.

Some people are so connected to, and comfortable with, their responses that the mere suggestion they have the ability to change them can be emotionally overwhelming. Indeed, no matter how destructive and unproductive those patterns may be, remaining in them may appear less daunting, and even preferable. What they don't yet realize is that reframing a response can have an immediate impact on one's energy and vibrations, which could assist with attracting positive energy and abundance into their world.

Al would come in each week and tell me he was not meant to be happy. His relationships never worked out; every time he had some money put aside something "big" happened and he would have to spend it; and his father was miserable and constantly put him down. Al was so stuck in the story he had created for himself that he was not supposed to be happy that each situation he encountered served as justification, validation, and support for it.

Remember, whatever story you put out into the Universe is what you will live out and, ultimately, become.

During our sessions, we worked on reframing Al's story. He told stories of his father's abusive background and he realized the role model his father had for parenting was unhealthy and dysfunctional. As a result, he struggled with depression and alcoholism and wasn't able to give the support and love as a parent to him that he never received himself. We talked about his father's behavior as an opportunity for him to learn to love himself and be okay with his own choices, rather than seeking the approval from his father that would never come. We talked about the series of unsatisfying relationships in his life, including with women, as a reflection of the same lesson and we used it as an opportunity for him to change the story his father was passing on to him. With coaching and guidance, Al was also able to change his story about money and was amazed to find that when something big inevitably came up he had the money put aside to do so.

Over time, and with his willingness to do so, Al was able to view his life circumstances from a different perspective, freeing him from the self-doubts, anger and resentments he had learned while growing up. He was able to see himself as a powerful man who overcame obstacles life threw his way and was able to find peace and happiness. He rose to the challenge to create success in his life, thereby rejecting the legacy and suffering the same fate as the rest of his family line. In working with my clients in this way, they become empowered with the notion that they do have choices in how they process information and respond.

As mentioned earlier, many people don't yet realize that they have any say in the matter at all. And when they say, "I don't have a choice," what they really mean is that they feel they must stay in the stuck place they are in because the alternatives that would create change are too overwhelming to consider. These changes may feel very "high risk," simply because they are unknown. We've all heard the adage, "The devil you know is better than the devil you don't." Well, many people take it to heart and let it rule their lives until they move out of a story of victimization and allow their view and meaning of that story to change. Like most rules, "The Rules" I have been given intuitively over the course of my career as a healer offer safety, protection, order – all of which assist in creating an ideal environment for people to coexist. The Rules provided in this book work as guidelines to ensure that you are focusing on that over which you have control: you.

When we feel a lack of control over our circumstances, the tendency is to "deflect," or put the responsibility for change on others in our world. While this appears to "work" at first because it takes the pressure off us to keep "trying," it inevitably creates resentments, guilt, shame, anger, exhaustion, depression, anxiety and overall general chaos.

Here is how the reframing process works. First, you need to have a willingness to accept that, in any situation, you have a choice. You also must be willing to change your perception that you have the right to judge, demand change from, or make comments to anyone who isn't doing what you feel they should be doing or who has wronged you. You need to let go of the notion that you are entitled to behave any way you see fit as a result of being "wronged." When you accept that you are not, under any circumstances, entitled to tell other people what they must do and focus only on yourself and your choices, you will notice a shift in your world. Over time you will begin to notice a shift in your energy and mindset as you slowly take back the power over your own life. You will then be able to rewrite the negative story you have been telling yourself and shift from a victim of circumstance to someone who has unlimited potential and choices. Embracing this process will raise your vibrations, allowing you to become empowered and, ultimately, the fullest version of yourself. The choice and power to change are *always* yours.

Activity Practice the Power of Reframing

Reframing is probably the most challenging and emotionally draining of The Rules process. The more intense the emotions experienced during the particular event, the more of a struggle you will encounter in the process of attempting to reframe it. It is also in these most challenging exercises that you will find the most opportunity for growth. The word "opportunity" is, in and of itself, a reframe. In this space, reflect on some of the biggest "challenges" in your life and begin to think about what "opportunities" they provide for your personal learning and growth. Remember, the more intensely you are impacted by the emotion associated with the event, the greater the opportunity for your healing.

CUT THE SHIT

_____
_____
_____
_____
_____
_____
_____
_____
_____
_____
_____
_____
_____
_____
_____
_____
_____
_____
_____
_____
_____
_____
_____
_____
_____
_____
_____
_____
_____
_____

KEY DEFINITIONS

Before getting deeper into The Rules and the process of working through them, it is necessary for you to understand the meanings of phrases and words I refer to.

Vibrations (the raising and lowering of)

The foundational concept here is that everything – including us – is made up of energy, which we produce, vibrate with, and emanate at a certain frequency. If we were to look at this vibrational frequency on a scale, we would see that while in a human body our souls are at the lowest end, the Creator is at the highest, and ascended masters, angels, and our loved ones who are no longer in physical form vibrate at various points in between. That said, as souls in physical bodies we have opportunities on a moment-to-moment basis to raise or lower our vibrational energy with the choices we make. Positive thoughts, actions, and behaviors will raise your vibration, resulting in a closer connection to your higher energetic self and the spiritual realm. Emotions, thoughts, and actions that result in lower vibrational energy such as shame, guilt, apathy, grief, anger, and vanity can keep you from connecting with your higher self and intuition, and from becoming the best version of yourself.

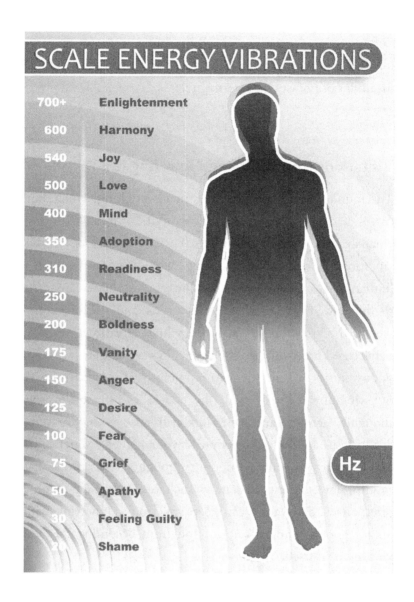

A Level Up or a Level Down

You've probably noticed that I often refer to "levels" – for example, a client that puts themselves in a position of "one level up" or "one up." Note that I am referring in these cases to a *self-imposed* hierarchy. Spiritually we are all on the same "level," so in that sense one's behaviors, thoughts, accomplishments, and actions do not make them better or worse than anyone else. In the human world, however, we tend to think of ourselves and others as occupying places in a power structure. When you look down on someone and/or allow yourself to perceive you are better than them, you place yourself on a higher rung in the hierarchy. By the same token, you take yourself down a rung, or level, whenever you agree that you deserve to be or are "less than" someone else.

Universal Law #8: The Law of Free Will

Of the twenty universal laws, this is one of the most important and serves as the foundation for our ability to utilize the others. This law states that "You always have free will to mitigate the impact of the event, or to transcend it entirely."

PART II

The Rules

Rule #1

Take Your Own Inventory

Redirect the energy you have been focusing on what you think others are doing wrong and/or their faults to understanding your own actions.

I've discussed this principle several times already, and with good reason: it is foundational to the process, the rule every other in this guide refers back to. Rule 1. As I mentioned, it is far easier to focus on what everyone else is doing wrong and how they are disappointing you than to identify and put energy into your own healing and betterment. In the world of magic (or chicanery) this is referred to as "sleight of hand," meaning perpetrating an illusion with one hand so another person doesn't notice what is happening with the other. In psychotherapy, it is called deflection, and is a form of self-protection. Either way, the person you are really deceiving is yourself. People often engage in this behavior when they perceive other solutions to their problems as emotionally draining, embarrassing, traumatic, painful, and anxiety-provoking. Again, sometimes the true source of anxiety is their fear of the unknown.

Deflection is an attempt to raise one's status (put themselves in a "one-up" position) when they are feeling "less than," but what it actually does is generate lower-vibrational thoughts and feelings associated with recognizing vulnerabilities and confronting inner struggles.

Often people justify deflection by picking someone they perceive is an "easy target" – meaning they are passive, avoid confrontations, and won't fight back. The easy target may be someone who already struggles with self-esteem and self-respect issues, so having blame placed on them is familiar. They may even have a disability such as Down's Syndrome or an emotional struggle such as anxiety or depression. Deflecting blame and/or attention onto them can appear less obvious and more satisfying.

It is also not unusual to deflect or pick on someone close to you and who you perceive loves you unconditionally so there is less risk of losing them in your life. An example of this would be a husband who blames his wife, who is struggling with depression, for having a messy house – this, to deflect attention away from the fact that he has been coming home late each evening because he's having an affair. Another common strategy is to pick on someone who has little consequence in your life and/or is not in your immediate support network, thereby reducing the risk of others in your circle noticing your behavior.

The bottom-line is that the deflector gives themselves permission to point out someone else's faults and demand they change them. This process, as mentioned earlier, has also been called "taking someone's inventory." Other examples of taking someone else's inventory include making a mental list of what you feel another person has done wrong, is not good at, or has vulnerability around. In addition to making that person feel badly, the inventory-taker may even share these faults or frailties with others.

There is any number of reasons someone gives themselves permission to treat others in this manner but, again, I've found it usually occurs when the person feels their trust has been broken due to the disrespectful or hurtful acts of another – i.e. being cheated on, stolen from or gossiped about – whether these events actually occurred or not. Sometimes they are deflecting to hide something else they are doing wrong, as in the example above, where the cheating husband berates his wife for the messy home; he too is likely acting out of some hurt he can't face. Whatever the case, the deflector's own wounding serves as justification for their behavior. What results is low-vibrational energy, guilt, anxiety, depression, embarrassment, anger, and the loss of relationships.

When working with a client who engages in deflection, the goal is to get them to recognize their behavior and turn their focus and energy away from others and back where it belongs: on themselves. In doing so they can take their own inventory, resolve their issues in a healthy way, and raise their vibration. Keep this objective in mind as you go through the rest of The Rules. How do you react when you feel someone (or life) has wounded you?

Rule #2

Don't "Should" All Over Yourself (Or Others)

The word should is an attempt to use guilt as a motivator. You are trying to manipulate someone into doing something you want and if they don't you will make them feel as badly as possible. Or you may be feeling low and unconsciously believe that bringing another down to your level will make you less so. This is what people mean when they say, "Misery loves company." I call it "shoulding all over someone," and it's a way of telling them they are not meeting your expectations. Once you determine that someone isn't meeting your expectations it is difficult to change that internal messaging; therefore, you give yourself permission to feel angry, resentful, minimized, guilty, victimized, entitled and depressed. Consequently, you also risk having the person you "should" on feel the same emotions.

Telling someone what they should be doing also implies that you are in the position of authority, creating a power differential in your relationship. Your way is the right way, and any noncompliance is a violation, enabling your low-vibrational emotions and thoughts. You create an internal ledger of unpaid debts, similar to the one Bob Cratchit had in "A Christmas Carol," and any time someone does not meet your expectations you add it to the list. Eventually, the debt grows so large that it would be nearly impossible to "pay off," no matter how hard the other person tries.

Should statements are often an attempt to have one's needs met. When you lay guilt on someone, you are allowing them to feel the weight of your disappointment, just as you feel disappointed by them. Examples of these statements include, "If you love me you 'should' want to spend Christmas with my family" and "A real man should come to my rescue if another man is trying to hit on me." Another example is, "I should get the promotion because I'm better qualified than he is." Sometimes the "should" is implied, yet it is still aggressive and conveys the message that the only correct viewpoint and/or action is yours.

Should is also a weapon we turn on ourselves when we feel bad or obligated to do something we don't want to do or feel is right for us. The internal dialogue is different, but the result is the same: low-vibrational energy and emotions.

Kerry, a client of mine, was caring for her dying mother in her own home – something she clearly expressed was her duty (and choice) to do so. She had engaged in a conflict with her best friend who had decided she could not care for her own aging father and instead elected to put him into a nursing home. Kerry processed their interactions during her sessions, expressing anger and disgust with her friend who, in her mind, was not doing what she deemed to be the "right" thing by her parent. "It is an honor to care for your elders," she told me, "and she should be caring for her dad herself." She and her friend were getting into heated and uncomfortable arguments, in which she negated her friend's right to make the best choice for herself and her father. Kerry was "shoulding" so frequently and so adamantly that it was threatening the foundations of their friendship.

As mentioned, you can also try to motivate yourself through "shoulding." Examples of such statements include, "I should be cleaning instead of watching TV" or "I shouldn't eat this." Whether you wind up doing what you "should" or not, you are stirring up low-vibrational energy that has no benefit and, over time, can have serious negative impacts on your spirit, mind, and body.

Some people are convinced that if not for "shoulding" themselves they would never get anything done. They fear they would become unproductive and/or irresponsible – their home would be messy; they wouldn't exercise or eat right and would be unhealthy/overweight; they wouldn't do their homework, etc. Moreover, they fully attribute any successes and accomplishments to the "shoulding"; essentially, they pile on the guilt until there is no choice but to do the task they would otherwise struggle with.

Some people recognize their "shoulding" but find it difficult to get out of this negative loop. Others defend it, arguing that their expectations (of themselves and others) and feelings are important and it is not inherently unhealthy to request what you want or need. It is also not unhealthy to recognize behaviors or thoughts that do not support your own goals. In fact, they say, presenting your requests, needs and values promotes appropriate communication and boundaries.

While it *is* considered good boundary and energy maintenance to express your concerns, frustrations and disappointments, it is *not* healthy to do so in a manner that is aggressive and lowers your own vibrations. For example, instead of saying to yourself, "I shouldn't be watching TV, the house is a mess and I should be cleaning instead," you could tell yourself, "The house feels better to me when it is clean, so I'll clean for two hours and then allow myself time to watch TV." Rather than tell someone, "If you really loved me you should come with me to my parents' house for Christmas" you might say instead, "It would really mean a lot to me if you would come to Christmas dinner with my family." In each case, the first statement attempts to motivate with guilt or "shaming," while the other focuses on a positive goal or result.

Rule #3

You Don't Have the Right to Invalidate How Another Person is Thinking

Think back to a time when someone expressed a thought or feeling that you felt was not completely truthful. Perhaps you felt they were exaggerating to be manipulative in some way, for example, a coworker who you believe faked being sick so they could leave work early or a friend who exaggerated how upset they were about a breakup because they wanted attention. It can be frustrating when it seems someone is not being completely truthful about what they are feeling for some sort of personal gain or to manipulate you; it can also be difficult to not call them out on it, especially if others also seem to see the truth and stay silent. It is as if it's more important to ignore the behavior and avoid conflict than to openly note the discretion.

Take this one step further. Can you recall a time when someone told you something you said or did that made them feel bad? Essentially, they are telling you did something "wrong." If you're like most of us, you experienced embarrassment, anger, depression, and guilt when this person expressed hurt or humiliation over your behavior towards them. And if you're like most people, your natural and first reaction was to defend yourself, or to respond with denial in an effort to deflect responsibility. You might even accuse the other person of being deceptive or purposefully manipulative. For example, if someone says, "You hurt my feelings when you accused me of not caring about where you wanted to go for dinner," you might respond with, "That did not hurt your feelings. You never care where we go for dinner so I didn't ask this time." Another example would be if a coworker felt disrespected when you told a distasteful joke and filed a complaint about you. If you're violating this rule you might try to discredit their feelings by saying, "We tell each other dirty jokes all the time and you always laugh. That didn't really upset you; you just wanted to get back at me for (fill in the blank)."

Sometimes people will assume what someone else is thinking or feeling and relay this to others, which can lead to a skewed version of a story and perhaps hurtful rumors as well. I remember an interaction with a coworker, who told me, "Mary really likes Trump." Now, I knew this coworker was vehemently opposed to Trump and what he stands for, and was attempting to stir the pot and perhaps get me to be as outraged with Mary as he was. Curious as to what had really transpired between them, I asked Mary about the conversation. "I never said I did or did not like Trump," she replied. "We were having a discussion about how things are portrayed in the media and I said reporters generally tell the side of any story that supports their position. At no time did I say anything about how I personally felt about Trump." In this example the coworker assumed what Mary was thinking, and misrepresented that to me, leading to inaccurate statements that could potentially create a toxic work environment, one in which a person felt ostracized for their political views.

I hear this sort of "gaslighting" all the time in my work with couples. One person expresses how they were feeling or what their intentions were, only to be accused of lying by the other. In one session the husband said, "You embarrassed me when you pointed out how many drinks I've had in front of my friends." His wife's reaction – "Oh please! I didn't embarrass you. You don't care what your friends think" – completely invalidated his feelings. In another example, a woman told her partner, "I felt so betrayed. Didn't you notice I stopped talking to everyone and left for three hours?" The partner's response: "You left because you wanted an excuse to go golfing. You are just saying that now so I won't be upset that you went golfing again."

Telling someone they are lying about their experience implies that 1) you actually have more knowledge about their feelings than they do; and/or 2) they are being deceptive about their feelings; and/or 3) their feelings are invalid. People can defend this strategy by saying they know what the other person said was a lie, and that they only said it in an attempt to assign blame or deflect their own actions.

Defer to Rule #1: Play in your own sandbox. If you give yourself permission to assume others are being deceptive because you can "just tell," you are putting yourself in a position of power over them and, ultimately, driving a wedge between you. No one wants to be honest about their feelings, wants or desires if they know you're only going to belittle or discredit them for it. Essentially you discourage honest and open communication by telling others they cannot trust you.

When I point out this behavior to a client the most common defense I hear is that they are simply stating "the truth." They say things like, "I'm usually right," in reference to their assumptions about the other person, or "I know him/her better than anyone else so I know what they really meant." Don't misunderstand me here: the person may be completely justified in accusing the other person of lying. What I am saying is that if you know someone has a habit of regularly being manipulative or lying about their feelings, either find a way to end the relationship or spend less time in their presence. Continually pointing out that you are accurate in your observations is not likely to fix or lessen this behavior.

Oftentimes discrediting what someone says about their feelings and/or their intentions is another effort to deflect and absolve yourself of responsibility. In telling someone you didn't actually hurt their feelings, embarrass them, disrespect them, or otherwise make them feel bad, you are avoiding examining your own behavior or doing any work to change it. Also, you may be reinforcing the notion that you are, once again, a victim.

Rule #4

The Actions of Others
Do Not Justify Yours

Consider this scenario. Your child is being physically and emotionally bullied by another. Would you tell your child to hit back, or would you tell them that being hit does not give them the right to retaliate? When I was growing up, if someone put their hands on you and you did the same, you were seen as acting in self-defense and only the instigator was disciplined (or certainly given the more severe punishment).

In the modern education system, the response has been to discipline anyone involved in any sort of incident where any type of violation of school policy occurs. This change occurred as a result of a shift in focus to one's free will. Putting your hands on someone (aside from blocking blows), regardless of what they did to you first, does not absolve you of responsibility to manage your own actions. Yet, some disagree, and tell me they instruct their children to defend themselves by hitting back. Their thought is 1) if someone hits you first you need to defend yourself; 2) if you don't "fight" back you will get a reputation for being weak and you will keep being bullied. They also may tell their children that if they physically defend themselves they may get in trouble in school but not at home.

These parents are looking at the issue only in the moment, without considering the bigger picture. In that moment, their child is being bullied and they need it to stop. Now, any parent will tell you this is a horrible situation and that their first and only priority is the safety of their child. Their solution is for their child to show the bully there are consequences, and everyone else they are not weak or to be messed with.

This is another example of a "solution" that initially appears successful but creates bigger problems in the long run. Yes, fighting back may indeed deter that bully; however, there is always a bigger kid who wants to challenge the "winner," which can lead to more physical altercations. The message the bullied child learns is that it is acceptable to harm another being if you believe you have been wronged or your rights violated. This can create a sense of entitlement that, as mentioned earlier in this book, can impact many other behaviors and choices throughout someone's life, creating larger issues. Please note that I am not trying to "solve" the bullying problem, as this is a complex and pervasive issue, with circumstances unique to each family. What I am saying is that when a child (or anyone) puts their hands on someone in aggression they are giving themselves permission to engage in lower-vibrational energy that can have long-lasting effects on their internal and external environments.

Recall that entitlement is one of the most common "solutions" that tend to backfire on us, either immediately or in the long run. One gentleman told me how he had gone to his wife's job to tell her boss that she was having an affair with a coworker.

In that moment he was so angry and humiliated that he thought only of making her feel humiliated as well. The result was far worse: both his wife and her coworker were fired for breaking a company rule against dating people in the workplace. Although he had achieved his immediate goal of embarrassing her, he brought suffering as well, as she could no longer afford to pay her half of the living expenses. Still, he refused to acknowledge that chaos he had brought about, saying only that, "She deserved it." Several months after the incident, they broke up.

In one session, Bill and his husband Mark were telling a story about an argument they'd had over the weekend. Bill was very angry when Mark took all his clothing and dumped it in the middle of their driveway, making a scene in their front yard and embarrassing him in front of their neighbors. When it was Mark's turn to speak, his response was a very typical one: "Did you ask him what he did first?" People tell themselves it is perfectly acceptable for them to do something that would otherwise be offensive so long as they perceive they have the "right" to. Essentially, they weigh the awfulness of the other person's behavior, respond in kind and, when challenged, say, "Well, he did it first!" Like the bullied child who is counseled to defend themselves, they are "hitting back" to avoid the appearance of vulnerability.

Let me be clear here. I am certainly not saying someone doesn't have the right to be upset when their vulnerabilities are triggered. What I am saying is that while pain is inevitable, suffering is optional. Justifying your own poor behavior as self-defense lowers your vibrations, threatening your own health of spirit, mind and body. It implies you have no responsibility for, and cannot be expected to control, your own reaction. It also implies you are a victim. When you lash out, you are likely reacting not only to the current situation but many like it that have left you in this very familiar place. It is that place of feeling disrespected and minimized that you vowed you would never allow yourself to be in again.

You likely have also decided you will not allow the other person the satisfaction of "getting away with" what they have done to you. Again, whomever you are currently having a conflict with is likely bearing the brunt of all the emotions you have experienced in similar situations throughout your life. Remember though, that, "An eye for an eye makes the whole world blind." In the moment you may feel temporary relief from your pain, but ultimately you have lowered your own vibrations and contributed to a chasm between you and the people in your life.

Rule #5

You Don't Get to Be Angry at Them for What You *Think* They Really Mean

Have you ever been talking with someone and they said something that caught you the wrong way? You ask them to repeat it, and it doesn't sound any better the second time. You try to give them the benefit of the doubt, but you can't shake the feeling that what they said sounded condescending, rude, disrespectful, accusatory, angry, or just plain hurtful. When you point-blank tell them how upsetting it was to you, they reply, "I didn't mean it like that," and that's when the argument begins. You tell them you know EXACTLY what they meant and are pissed about it; they insist you are misreading what they said and may also accuse you of "overreacting."

People are a work in progress. They can be working on habits they need to correct. When someone is actively working on changing a response that is a habit for them, they struggle with making this change stick consistently. This is a normal part of the change process. For example, Bill had a bad habit of reacting angrily when he perceived someone was trying to control or question him. With some work, he was able to identify this as a trigger from his abusive childhood, with his controlling parents consistently giving him the message that he couldn't be trusted. Although Bill was able to recognize and understand his reactions, this was only the first part of what he needed to do to begin changing this behavior. When he was having a good day, he was able to quickly get control of his reaction. On other days, when he was triggered while also struggling with other influences, he would fly off the handle and only realize what he had done after some time had passed.

We often invited his wife, Tracy to participate in the sessions so she would be aware of what he was working on. They recounted to me a recent argument they had gotten into after something she said upset him. Tracy in turn accused him of "doing what you always do" – referring to his quick temper – after which she said he rolled his eyes, said something under his breath and slammed the door as he walked out of the room. This, in her mind, was evidence that Bill hadn't changed and was still being abusive. He defended himself, saying he had not done any of the things she accused him of. In his mind he was very mindful of his response and did walk away quickly, but only to diffuse the situation. Tracy accused him of lying to cover up the fact that he was, in fact, engaging in his "old behaviors." They argued for the remainder of the session, with them going back and forth about his intentions and actions. By this time he had done quite a bit of work on himself and was very distraught that she didn't see it. Furthermore, when he told her "That wasn't what I was thinking or doing at all," she put a great deal of energy into supporting her belief that he was lying.

When someone has a history of behaving a certain way, it is normal to assume they haven't changed, even when they are in fact making progress. It becomes an issue when they explain that progress and you fire back in an attempt to get them to admit they are lying or inaccurate. In this case, Tracy gave herself permission to tell her husband what his intentions and actions really meant and to be angry with him for it, no matter what he said.

As mentioned earlier, people often defend this behavior by saying that when they think someone is being deceptive they are "usually proven right." They are referring back to that ledger of faults again; they feel they know the other person so well that they have the right to make the determination that they are being deceptive. Typically, this leads to a hurtful back and forth with people defending their position rather than focusing on the topic that led to the argument in the first place. Also, the person who accuses the other of being deceptive is often attempting to put themselves into the "one-up" position we have discussed previously, which inevitably disrupts the healthy balance between them and creates further conflict and dysfunction. Essentially, the whole dynamic generates and perpetuates low-vibrational thoughts, feelings and behaviors for all involved.

When we interact with others frequently it is normal to develop assumptions about their motivation and motives, resulting in repeated experiences. For example, Liz and John got into a heated exchange when, after telling his wife about a business venture he was working on, John perceived that she rolled her eyes and sucked her teeth. John began to go into a tirade about how she never supports him, doesn't listen to him, and frequently reacts dismissively when he attempts to discuss these types of subjects with her. Liz immediately started yelling over him that she hadn't done any of what he said. This argument went on for several minutes, with him telling her she was passive-aggressively doing "what you always do" and he therefore had every right to scream at her. She insisted that he had made a mistake and was quite insulted by his overreaction.

Similar to previous examples, Liz was attempting to tell him that she wasn't feeling what he told her she was feeling, while he justified his reaction (yelling) by insisting he knew that she was lying. The danger here is the same as when one violates Rule #4: believing yourself entitled to react poorly because of what you *think* others mean implies you are the true authority on their thoughts and feelings. Furthermore, when the "accused" is in the process of recognizing and changing their own behaviors, assuming from past interactions that they are "doing it again" can have a negative impact on their progress and healing.

This can also come up when we act based on generalizations, whether it is true of a particular person or not. For example, if a man's past experiences tell them that "women do not support any ambitions that aren't their own," he can then apply this notion to every woman he comes into contact with, assuming she will disrespect his dreams or desires. The message of this rule: be careful about making assumptions. Remember, "to assume is to make an ass of 'u' and me!"

Rule #6

You Don't Get to Tell Others How They Should Feel or How They Are Feeling

At first glance this rule appears to be saying the same thing as Rule #3, "You Don't Have the Right to Invalidate How Others are Feeling." However, unlike Rule #3, this rule refers to telling someone how they "should" feel and then becoming upset at them when you assume they aren't feeling that way. The difference is subtle, yes, but significant.

In the movie *Star Trek Into Darkness,* Uhura accuses Spock of not caring about her feelings, saying, "Good thing you don't care about dying... You didn't feel anything.... You didn't care." She concluded, based on his lack of outward emotion, that he wasn't concerned with what happened to her and was resentful and angry at him for it. In typical Spock fashion, he replied:

> Your suggestion that I don't care about dying is incorrect... I had experienced those feelings before, multiplied exponentially the day my planet was destroyed... Such a feeling is something I choose never to experience ever again... You mistake my choice not to feel as a reflection of my not caring...While I assure you the truth is precisely the opposite.[1]

---

[1] To watch this scene, check out: www.youtube.com/watch?v=w6E8b20Iz5E

In a couple's session, Melanie was emotionally falling apart as she talked about how she had been crying all the time and was either not sleeping or struggling to sleep through the night. It had become clear to her their relationship was not working out and they may need to break up. She noted her partner "didn't care at all," saying he slept soundly through the night, didn't cry at all, and overall didn't show any signs of being upset. He was very hurt by her accusation and tried to explain that he was just as upset as she was; he just didn't deal with things the same way.

This scenario occurs frequently. Someone focuses their energy on assuming that the other person isn't as upset about the event as they "should" be, which can quickly turn into, "You never really loved me anyway." In this example Melanie has given herself permission to scream at her partner, based on her assumption about his feelings for her throughout their entire relationship.

Many people assume what they think and feel and how they express and experience emotions is the same as everyone else does (or should do). And, as many assumptions, this is a misconception that results in misunderstandings and arguments.

For example, Fred grew up in a family that rarely spent time together outside of major life events. His partner's family, on the other hand, spent a great deal of time together and she spoke with her mother daily. They were also expected to show up for family dinner every week and go on vacations with her family, which left Fred feeling trapped and under a great deal of pressure. He told her he could tell she was feeling the pressure as well but went along with it because she felt too guilty to go against her parents. She insisted they had a healthy and close family and cherished how much time they spent together. As a result of his own perceptions and experiences, he was essentially telling her she was lying, and that her family interactions were unhealthy because they didn't match his own. This led to a range of emotions and several arguments based on misunderstandings that didn't need to happen.

We often conclude that if someone's experiences do not match our own they are unhealthy, irresponsible, disrespectful, rude, or even deviant. At best, engaging in this type of thought process is naive and shortsighted, causing misunderstandings, hurt feelings, and unnecessary arguments. At its worst, assuming without evidence what people are feeling can lead to the demise of what could have been a happy relationship.

Some people, particularly empaths, can wear their hearts on their sleeves. They intuitively know that it's natural and even healthy to fully express their feelings so as to get them "out" of the body, as well as to get needed support from others. Other people, however, are "stuffers," meaning they push down whatever they are feeling deep into their consciousness and thus avoid dealing with it. Still others are fully aware of what they are feeling, and although they are experiencing and processing their emotions in a healthy way, they have no need to express them aloud and may appear to be feeling nothing at all.

The point is, you cannot readily assume that whatever someone expresses in body language, tone/volume of voice, et cetera, is a true representation of how they are feeling inside. Instead of assuming, you would be wise to simply ask them how they are feeling. You may very well learn that they are in fact not experiencing the same emotions you are about something and – you can guess what comes next – you don't have permission to tell them how to feel or make their reaction "wrong." Ask them to explain how they are feeling, reframing a negative interaction as an opportunity to grow and be supportive.

Rule #7

If You Are Accusing Me of Something, You Are Likely Guilty of the Same Thing

Reflect back on Rule #1: Play in Your Own Sandbox. If you are putting energy into telling other people they are (in your opinion) wrong, then once again you have made a decision to engage in emotional policing. We have already concluded that telling others how/where/when they "should" be is a foul ball. Have you ever heard the saying that if someone accuses another person of poor behavior they are likely engaging in that same behavior themselves? In my experience it has been proven accurate time and time again. In fact, I know of many fellow therapists and coaches who tend to follow this line of thinking when assessing their own clients.

For example, if a client tells me they are distraught about their partner's behavior that seems to indicate cheating, I feel it's prudent to assess any similar behavior in the client. When I point out that their "evidence" is really based on assumptions, I pretty much hear that same rationale: "I'm pretty good at reading people and picking up on these things and I'm usually right." Could this be true? Of course, but it's just as, if not more, likely that the client is recognizing similar behaviors in themselves. Universal law states that "Like attracts like," which means that whatever energy and cycles you engage in will likely draw others with those same patterns. In other words, the behavior you feel is unacceptable in someone close to you is probably something you're doing as well.

I was working with Steve on his need for validation from others, which had impacted various relationships throughout his lifetime. He had been coming to me, on and off, for years to talk about unresolved issues in his marriage, and that session was no different. In fact, he spent most of his energy focusing on how he felt his wife didn't actually want to be happy and wouldn't entertain any suggestions to improve their marriage. He said she was too busy being the victim and preferred to look for reasons to be angry and resentful rather than make changes.

As he spoke, I couldn't help but notice that Steve was doing the same thing: playing victim to his wife but never making moves to get out of or change the relationship, and I challenged him to consider this. We discussed his acceptance of a lifetime role as a man who deserved to be belittled by others, women in particular. This pattern had played out both in his relationship with his mother and family of origin and it was a role he elected to continue in his marriage. Moreover, he was accusing his wife of the same victimization and apathy he, in fact, was engaging in.

Another client, Debbie spent session time telling me how her husband had married her under false pretenses. When they dated, and for a short time following their marriage, they were caught up in the energy of the new relationship. His attention was mostly focused on her, and he prioritized her needs, sometimes above his and certainly above those of his children from his previous marriage. He acted like the man she had always wanted. Shortly after the wedding, however, his focus and priorities changed drastically. He was now putting almost no time into planning for or spending any time with her and seemed to put all his energy into pleasing himself and his children. Debbie felt he took their marriage, and her, for granted. She even went so far as to accuse him of purposefully misleading her.

I pointed out her husband could easily accuse her of the same "deception." When they were first married, she had spent a lot of quality time with his children, planning family activities and putting a great deal of energy into making them feel welcomed and comfortable – all of which her husband found very endearing. Within a short time, however, she was engaging with his children less and less, until she literally refused to have anything to do with them, telling her husband they weren't her responsibility, and he should find a babysitter.

Now, do I believe Debbie purposefully misled her husband into thinking she was going to be the perfect stepmother? No. I think she absolutely went into the situation with the best possible intentions of forming a new, happy family. However, she soon came to struggle with the differences in their parenting styles, and her limited ability to guide and discipline them. She also felt he had come to expect her assistance and that she was putting more effort into their upbringing than he was, which resulted in her resentment and complete withdrawal. Judging from the way he had behaved in their early days together, she now felt misled. Of course, her husband too may have made a similar argument – that he had married her thinking she wanted to be a mother figure to his children, only to learn that was not the case.

While there are many circumstances that can change the dynamics of a relationship after marriage, the notion that one intentionally misled the other beforehand is often not an accurate one. Of course, there are people who misrepresent themselves in an effort to secure a mate, however, in my experience most of the time this is simply not the case. My point is, Debbie was accusing him of engaging in behaviors that she believed were purposefully deceptive, unaware that those same thoughts could be applied to her own actions as well.

A common response when I point out that this rule has been violated is, "It's different." In other words, most people give themselves permission to engage in poor behavior while having very little tolerance for others doing the exact same thing. This once again takes us back to Rule #1, which is all about taking responsibility only for what you are saying and doing. Taking inventory of someone else's behavior only creates emotions and vibrations that can lead to negative impacts on spiritual, physical and mental health.

Rule #8

Don't Give Yourself Permission to Be "One Up"

Simply put, this rule states that you never have the right to consider yourself superior to any other living creature. If I tell myself I am better than someone else I then become entitled to engage in negative and judgmental thinking about that person and/or behave in a way that negates their basic rights as a being.

Jane spent a great deal of energy in her sessions talking about the situations that arose whenever she and her best friend, Susan, got together with their children. Jane felt Susan was too passive in her parenting strategies, which to Jane was apparent in the way Susan's kids acted around her own. In fact, Jane's children had begun to see her as the "bad guy." She was to the point where she felt as if they needed to end their friendship and was angry with Susan for putting them in this position. Furthermore, Jane frequently focused on how irresponsible Susan was, noting how her own children would "never act like that" because she would never allow it. Jane was making herself the superior parent and placing her friend into a "one down" position, which allowed her to absolve herself of responsibility for their friendship ending.

I have found people tend to see things as black or white – "all good" or "all bad" with little to no room for situations or behaviors in between. People also tend to label their own thoughts and behaviors on the highest and most "right" end of a scale, placing others they don't see eye-to-eye with on the complete opposite end. This is how they justify putting them into a category of people at whom they can turn down their nose.

In the example above, Jane elected to see herself as the perfect parent, who always made the most appropriate choices with her children. Susan and, by extension, her children were the opposite, making it okay for Jane to judge their behaviors and hold onto a variety of lower-vibrational thoughts and feelings towards them. If she only could allow herself to see that her own parenting choices may fall far on the other extreme of a parenting scale, maybe she would be more open to talking about changing her thoughts and actions to meet her friend somewhere in the middle.

People tend to accuse others of making choices that resulted in a certain outcome, rather than reflecting on their own choices. Have you ever gotten into an argument with someone after they said, "If you hadn't done this, that wouldn't have happened"? They say it without tact or regard for your feelings, then get upset when you are offended and "start an argument," all because you "took it the wrong way." While it may be true that you could have responded differently to what was said, they could also have presented their sentiment in a different way or chosen not to say it at all. Everyone needs to be responsible for their own choices, including the words that come out of their mouths.

One thing that never fails to aggravate me is when someone says their partner "is like my third child," meaning the partner tends to focus more on themselves and/or does not think in terms of the "bigger picture." The thing to remember here is that we all have our own strengths and vulnerabilities, and we tend to get into relationships with people who have the opposite strengths and vulnerabilities. For example, someone who has a strength in self-care gravitates toward someone who tends to put the needs and desires of others first, sometimes at the expense of their own happiness. Someone who is more focused on being productive may be with someone who struggles with motivation. Someone who is good at managing money gets together with someone who is freer with spending, and so on.

Rather than understanding someone's actions as simply different from their own, people often see the behaviors as something that creates more work for them, leaving them to conclude the other person is wrong (irresponsible, irrational, insensitive, lacking common sense, et cetera). When someone comments that their partner is "like my other child," they are reacting from a place of anger, frustration, and overwhelm; they are feeling as if they aren't getting any help or understanding from their partner about how much work they already have to do. They are feeling invalidated. Saying they feel as if they "have another child" becomes the only way they feel they can get the other person to understand and, hopefully, change.

This is another example of how someone's intended solution creates a bigger problem. Telling someone they are acting like a child does not promote understanding at all; it provokes the other person into feeling belittled, emasculated, angry, invalidated, and hurt. If you truly want to have someone understand and validate you, start by providing exactly what you hope to get in return: empathy, vulnerability, validation, and cooperation. There is nothing wrong with you wanting to have all these things, the problem usually comes from how you attempt to get it.

The history books are filled with people whose feelings of entitlement and superiority to others have caused great wars, mass destruction, death, and suffering. Surrounding yourself with others who agree with you only fuels the notion that you are right. Holding on to feelings of superiority only leads to toxic emotions and lower-vibrational energy that get in the way of life's blessings.

Rule # 9

You Cannot Hold Anyone Responsible for the Actions of Another Person

Omnipotence is defined as "the state of being truly almighty and above all in every sense and aspect." People often put others so high on a pedestal that they expect omnipotence from them. When you place someone else at the center of your Universe, you also expect (and perhaps demand) that they take responsibility for the thoughts, feelings, and/or actions of everyone around them.

I was working with Dave and Rita, a married couple who frequently fought over how his mother spoke with and to her. The mother would make comments that Rita felt were passive-aggressive, disrespectful, and rude. In their couple's session, Dave and Rita processed an argument that had occurred after Rita demanded Dave confront his mother about her comments and "stand up for me." Furthermore, Rita had been so irate with him, it was as if he had made the offensive comments himself.

There are two different pieces to this situation. First, Dave agreed that his mother is condescending and rude, as well as disrespectful towards Rita, thereby validating her feelings. He also noted that he needed to deal directly with the situation by speaking with his mother in support of his wife. This is appropriate and healthy, however, the best way to handle this would be to first talk this through with his wife to plan for how he will address this with his mother. Many times, the partner who feels offended wants to tell the other person what they should say and how they should say it. They believe they are justified in this because of how they were treated. The problem with this is that the other spouse becomes a puppet, only doing what they are told and likely in a way that does not fit how they would normally manage situations. Again, it is best for them to talk it out together so is handled in a way that meets the needs of both.

The second piece to consider is Rita is placing responsibility for what her mother-in-law said, squarely on Dave's shoulders. Remember that one of the guiding principles of The Rules is that you and you alone are responsible for you. This being said, it is completely disrespectful, unhealthy, and illogical to hold someone responsible for the thoughts, actions, and feelings of a third person. Rita has given herself permission to speak down to Dave because of the sentiments spoken by his mother. Clearly his mother is being inappropriate, but she alone needs to be held accountable for her actions. In placing blame on Dave and giving herself permission to hold a grudge against him Rita is sabotaging any chance to heal the relationship.

This phenomenon often happens in blended families, which already tend to have growing pains as couples with children from other relationships attempt to form a new group dynamic. Children can test and push the boundaries, struggling to adjust to someone else playing the role of co-parent. This is a normal reaction to a situation these children feel they didn't have any control over. Sometimes, however, it can threaten and challenge the integrity of their parent's new relationship, thus it is not uncommon for these couples to enter into counseling for help. For example, the step-parent can become resentful, blaming their spouse for the actions of the children. Yes, parents are responsible for disciplining and guiding their children, however, it is irrational, unrealistic, and dangerous to ask them to take complete control over every word and act.

While some people expect someone in their life to be "omnipotent," some hold the belief that they are personally responsible for the thoughts, feelings, and actions of others. When you allow yourself to be solely responsible for what others think and feel there is a danger that you make choices based on how you perceive others would feel and/or react, rather than what you think is best for you. This results in a host of low vibrational thoughts and feelings whenever someone reacts negatively to something you say or do.

I had a client, Rick, who would say yes to everything someone asked of him – be it helping them move, giving them a ride to the airport, donating to a charity, or buying something to support an organization. When I asked him in session why he never said no he admitted he "felt bad." He placed too much concern on others' feelings of overwhelm and anxiousness and wanted to do something that would allow them to successfully resolve those feelings. When someone upset him, he rarely confronted them, rationalizing that he was a "strong person" and would rather handle it himself than risk making them uncomfortable or hurt. Over time this habit of internalizing his own hurt and lower-vibrational emotions manifested as frequent headaches and other physical symptoms as his body struggled to manage what he was not expressing.

When you live in accordance with Rule #9, you understand no one can be expected to take responsibility for the thoughts and actions of others; therefore, you promote higher vibrations within yourself and consequently those around you. The importance of this cannot be emphasized enough when you are trying to manage your relationships, both personal and pro-fessional.

Rule #10

You Cannot Expect Someone to "Just Know" What You Need

I've found that many people put an expectation on themselves and/or others to adhere to an internal set of rules that govern behavior within relationships. They truly believe these rules are universally understood and accepted, and that when they are violated the wronged party is justified in doing and saying things that would not normally be considered acceptable, even according to those same rules! People often define "normal" and "healthy" by the rules and expectations they grew up with; anything that doesn't match what was modeled for them is considered a "problem"; "dysfunctional"; not how it "should" be; or "wrong."

When I am working with a client it often becomes apparent that they or someone they're involved with has a list of behaviors they believe others should know and follow. They say things like, "That's just what you do," or make statements that begin with "You should…" The most common examples involve the expectations people place on their partners, particularly when it comes to interacting with family. For example: "When it's my mother's birthday you are coming with me to her house (because that's "just what you do")." If the family is getting together to buy someone a present, you are expected to contribute, again, because that's just what you do. These people feel entitled to not only write the rules but put pressure on anyone who does not agree with or meet their expectations. The truth, as mentioned above, is that systems, familial and otherwise, make their own rules. No one else gets to decide what is "normal" and "healthy" for everyone else.

I was working with a woman, Fran, who was overwhelmed and exhausted from juggling a full-time job and parenting two small children. She expressed how angry she was with her husband John, who she felt was not helping with the household tasks. As an example, she told me that each night John would go to bed while she stayed up handwashing the baby bottles and preparing for the next day. Fran admitted she had not asked him for help in several months, nor had she told him about her growing anger and resentment. Eventually she exploded, screaming at John and telling him what a horrible father and husband he was.

Clearly, Fran didn't approach this conversation the best way, and it didn't go well. In her mind, it was John's job as husband and father to see how much she was doing and to jump in to help. When I suggested she let him know how overwhelmed she was and in need of his participation, she became furious with me. John "should" know he wasn't meeting expectations as a father and husband and offer help without her having to ask. She wanted him to notice what she was going through and just "do."

Please don't misunderstand me here. I am not saying it is wrong for someone to want help from their partner. What I am saying is that if you choose to not tell someone what you need, you are not entitled to expect them to "just know." No one is a mind-reader and certainly no one is born with an imprint of roles they simply step into.

Rule #10 also comes into play when people do things for others then get angry and resentful when the same or equivalent things are not reciprocated. One client told me she had paid for her friend's birthday to be put up on a Trinitron at a local baseball game but when it came time for her birthday the woman just texted, "Happy birthday." This experience led her down the proverbial rabbit hole of constantly being disappointed with others and not "getting what I give." In this case, the client was unconsciously supporting the cycle and story of her as a victim who no one ever thought of as special. She also acted in a way that allowed herself to stay aligned with that victimhood, as did the empathy she elicited from others.

Both personally and professionally I often hear people talk about what they do for others they are close to and how frequently frustrated, sad, and resentful they are when they don't receive that energy in return. For example, people who take the time to buy thoughtful gifts for others will get back "only an impersonal gift certificate"; people who make a "big deal" out of others' birthdays at home or work are sad when no one even remembers theirs. At Christmastime they fill their loved ones' stockings to the brim with carefully chosen trinkets, only to find their own is nearly empty. People who are always doing the driving when they go out complain that no one else ever offers to drive. People who babysit others' children are resentful that no one offers to "give them a break" from parenting. People who prepare someone's favorite meal may be surrounded by those who "hate to cook," and someone who gets up early to handle kids or pets so their partner can focus on a task or sleep gets angry that they never do the same.

Overall, people feel they should get back exactly what they do for others and react like a victim when this doesn't happen. And when others violate their rules by disagreeing with them or simply not complying, it leads to resentment, anger, and general dysfunction in the system. Oftentimes people get caught up in blaming or making judgments of others. There is no "let's agree to disagree"; they feel the need to define someone else as "wrong" so that they can feel more "right." The message here is that if you want to do something nice for someone, do so out of the goodness of your heart without the expectation of reciprocation. If you do things for others in hopes they will do the same for you, you may be setting yourself up for frequent disappointment and other, lower vibrational, emotions and experiences. Lastly, if you need help, do not expect someone else to read your mind, which leads us to the next rule.

Rule #11

Tell People What You Want, Not What You Don't Want

Have you ever noticed that people tend to put more focus and energy into what they don't want instead of what they do want? Do you do this? Think about it. If someone isn't giving you what you need or doing what you want, do you become angry and spend time saying how upset you are? It takes a great deal of energy to hold onto anger, resentment, and sadness, yet it often seems to be the natural inclination.

I'll explain this rule with a story that plays out in homes across the globe daily. Picture a child coming home with their school report card (or a test grade or something similar). Let's say the grade on this schoolwork is less than perfect, maybe even failing. It is common for a parent to respond in a way that is angry, punitive, and hurtful; they may even resort to disciplinary actions, depending on the situation. The response and discipline can go on for hours, days, weeks and even months. Did this happen when you were growing up? Have you experienced this with your own children? The energy from this exchange can be exhausting and overwhelming on all sides.

Now consider the opposite situation, where your child brings home an exceptional grade. You praise your child for their good work, telling him how proud you are of them. You may hang the report card or test on the refrigerator. You definitely put energy into celebrating the event, but how much time do you really spend on it? Was the awesome grade talked about for days and weeks to come? Did you spend as much time praising them and showering them with positive energy as you would have scolding them if the grade was failing? If not, you are not alone. This happens all the time, in all kinds of situations. Universal law tells us you will attract more experiences in your life that mirror the vibrations you put out there. If more people understood and lived by this law, they would have very different lives. In fact, the world would likely be a different place.

I have been working with Frank and Nancy for several years and they keep getting stuck in a pattern of focusing on what they don't want. Frank has a high-profile job with a high salary and often works upwards of sixty hours or more a week. Nancy used to have a career, but they had agreed she would quit her job to stay home to take care of the children and manage the household. Over the years there have been events that threatened the foundation of their marriage.

Each time they come back for therapy, Frank says the same thing: he doesn't feel that Nancy shows enough gratitude for him and what he does for their family. He's also quick to elaborate on what he feels she does that appears to be ungrateful. That part appears to be easy to talk about and when he does, they both leave feeling angry, resentful, and frustrated.

More than once, I have asked Frank to reflect on what kinds of things he would like from Nancy that would indicate she is grateful. This question stumps him every time. People are so conditioned to give examples of what they don't like; this takes little effort and puts no responsibility on them for whatever is happening. They are upset about getting what they don't want, but if you ask someone to talk about what their ideal situation would look like, they struggle to envision it.

In my experience there are a few common reasons people struggle with this rule. First, focusing on their victimhood allows them to justify being angry, resentful, unmotivated, rude, disrespectful, and sad. Let's say that, like Frank, you tell others how you work sixty-plus hours a week and your wife, who doesn't work, acts ungrateful. You get their sympathy, which reinforces the story you've been telling yourself. You may even begin to justify behaviors such as not coming home, drinking, and cheating. No one would blame you for making that choice after being treated so "poorly," right? And so you continue to play out the story that you are disrespected and unappreciated.

Here's the thing: if you never define and explain what types of interactions or behaviors would leave you feeling loved and appreciated, you cannot rationally expect others to give you what you want. However, when you are repeatedly asked what you want you have no answer because you never put any energy into identifying it. Instead, your focus has been on your role as victim, which may in fact be serving you in some way.

The second reason people may struggle with this rule is that they want to "teach someone a lesson." Consider the example about the parents' reaction to a less than desirable grade in school. Parents want to impress on children the disappointment associated with getting a bad grade or poor school report, their rationale being that the child will not want to repeat the scenario and strive to do better. I have found that parents employ this logic, but in my experience it often results in their kids growing up with a sense that they can never do anything right.

Consider the logic behind this strategy. You are giving more energy and focus to reminding someone of how they messed up and fell short of expectations. I am certainly not suggesting that parents never express disappointment or disapproval; however, I am suggesting that you may get a more favorable outcome if you also put an equal amount of energy into focusing on behaviors you want from your child. Reflect on your own childhood. Do you remember getting more attention for doing something you shouldn't? Maybe you always did the right thing and felt neglected while those (i.e., your siblings) who were "screw-ups" got all the attention. We have become so adept at catching children doing something wrong that we forget we can also catch them doing something right. Other people have told me that praising children will leave them always expecting others to say nice things to them, creating a "pansy" who's not "tough" enough. In response to this I will say the same as I do for each situation: everything in balance.

Rule #12

You Cannot Expect Another Person to Be Responsible for Meeting Your Unmet Childhood Needs

Have you ever heard the saying, "It takes a village to raise a child"? It refers to the notion that each being in your life is meant to be a blessing to you in a different way. We all have strengths and gifts we share with the world. Each individual in your life provides the opportunity for learning and growth in different ways and it is your job to sort out what those lessons are and learn them successfully.

To illustrate this, I encourage you to reflect on your own childhood. First, who comes to mind when I ask you who could you count on for "tough love"? This would be someone who always told you what you needed to hear instead of what you wanted to hear. This person never sugarcoated anything. You may have known this person reacted this way out of pure love for you and maybe struggled to say it directly (or just struggled with speaking with grace). Either way, if you went to this person you always knew what to expect.

Next, think about who you would go to if you just wanted someone who agreed with you, whatever your action or position, even if maybe you might have been wrong. You could always count on this person to back you up and defend you, no matter what. Moving on, think about trying to finish your math homework or an essay you needed help editing – who comes to mind? Now think about the person you could never please. No matter what you did they were never impressed, and you were unsuccessful at getting any praise from them. This person, believe it or not, was also there to assist your growth. They helped you to understand that you and you alone get to determine your self-worth. The point of this exercise is to show you that there is not usually one person in your world who meets all your needs. If you think about your life as an adult, you likely can identify many people who mirror those relationships, in the sense that each meets a different need.

We've all heard the term "honeymoon period" to describe the beginnings (usually the first twelve to eighteen months) of a romantic relationship. This is that exciting phase when couples are focused almost solely on each other, sometimes to the exclusion of others in their lives. Some, upon entering into a new relationship, feel like that person is their "everything," the one who meets all their needs. While this is natural in the beginning, over time it is not healthy or realistic to expect this of a partner, or to neglect your other relationships.

As I pointed out in the beginning, we all need multiple people in our network surrounding us, because each being (I'm including animals here too) has a purpose and place in our lives. Placing unrealistic expectations on one person sets up the relationship for failure, as the heaviness of those expectations inevitably violates boundaries and overwhelms the energy of the individuals and their bond.

This issue can become even more complicated if one or both members of the relationship have unmet needs from their childhood that they then "assign" the other. For example, if someone felt as if they were not made to feel important growing up, they can either consciously or unconsciously have an expectation of having this need met by their partner. If someone never felt they were loved unconditionally as a child, they may develop an insatiable desire to be loved that becomes toxic to the boundaries of the dynamics of the relationship. Any time there is an expectation that another person "needs to" or "should" meet certain needs for another person, the relationship will likely become toxic.

Stan grew up in an alcoholic home where the needs and actions of the alcoholic ruled the family. As an adult Stan struggled with the feeling that he would never find a relationship in which the other person considered his needs, and indeed he had a history of unsatisfying relationships that seemed to support this feeling. He consistently sabotaged relationships with women, money, and jobs as he played out the internal dialogue that he was unworthy and undeserving of love and abundance. The truth was he didn't regard his own needs but was resentful of others who he insisted were also disregarding him. After doing some work on recognizing where he was sabotaging himself, Stan did find a relationship he wanted to make work. Yet he still struggled with the balance of not allowing himself to be taken for granted while also not fully expecting his partner to fill the emotional holes left from his childhood.

The key element of this rule is to understand that no one else is responsible to meet your emotional, physical, and spiritual needs. It is easy to read this and object when you are in a relationship where there is an expectation the other person will provide love, support, and trust. While this is true, as is the case with the other rules, the key is balance. Your partner is not responsible to give you what you needed to get from your family of origin. If you felt lonely as a child, it is not your partner's job to provide companionship one hundred percent of the time. If you didn't feel anyone considered your needs as a child, it is not your partner's job to always put your needs first, even above their own, to make up for it.

When you didn't get basic needs met as a child, it can be tricky to understand what "normal" and "healthy" looks like in a relationship, because it was not modeled for you. This is why having the mindset that no one else is responsible for meeting your emotional needs is so critical to allowing the higher vibrational state that attracts and supports a healthy relationship. It ensures that when someone does meet these needs it is appreciated and valued, rather than expected.

Rule #13

You Don't Have the Right to Stop Trying, Even if You Believe You Have Tried "Everything"

I tend to see things on a graduated scale where I can describe them as mild, moderate, or severe. As mentioned, by the time most clients come for guidance and coaching they have been trying to resolve their issues (which they usually rate as moderate or severe) on their own for quite some time, with little or no success. What's interesting is that even when they come to me for my professional opinion and guidance, they often don't actually want to hear or use my suggestions (although if I point this out they likely don't recognize it).

Change is very difficult because it's uncomfortable and unfamiliar. This is why although most people say they want to experience something different the mere idea of making a change is frequently met with resistance. It's also why they'll continue to keep plugging away at the same own "solutions" that are not working and/or causing bigger problems. When I first start working with a client it is important to both identify the problem as noted by the client and what they have attempted in their efforts to solve it. Indeed, it is often within their attempted solutions that I find the key to where we need to begin developing different strategies.

As I stated previously, people also often come to me for help in figuring out how they can get other people in their lives to do what they want. This is when I hear things like, "I've tried everything" and "I made a bunch of changes and no one else has done anything"; "I've tried yelling, I've tried crying, I've tried asking reasonably, I've tried begging." Does this sound familiar?

Oftentimes, a person believes that he or she has tried every possible thing without success. They eventually give up, concluding that relief or resolution is out of reach. Typically, they have entitled themselves to believe 1) others in their lives have to make the changes since clearly the problem is not theirs and/or 2) they are not responsible for making any other changes since they have done everything and everyone else has done nothing and it is now everyone else's job to put in the effort ("It's your turn now, I'm done"). At this point I invite someone in my client's circle to join them in a session so this notion of "I've done everything and so it's everyone else's turn" can be played out in real-time. Most of the time the other party either feels the same way and can spell out all the efforts they feel they have put in while my client has changed nothing. This exercise helps drive home the realization that people see things from their own perspective, but neither or both of them are right or wrong.

Have you ever said to someone else (or has someone said to you) "If you didn't make such a big deal about this we wouldn't have fought about it"? Think about this for a minute. This statement is actually true and can be said to and about anyone and any situation. If two people are arguing because one made fun of the other, the argument from both people would be valid. "If you didn't make fun of me we wouldn't have had a fight"; "Well if you weren't so sensitive and didn't take everything so personally and could take a joke we wouldn't have fought." You could use this for any argument. Just about anyone at any time could make a choice that could change the course and outcome of any interaction. Many times, I find people want to avoid having a discussion about what they could do differently to improve a situation and prefer to create their own internal solution.

Tim was feeling as if his wife Lisa was spending too much time with her parents and considered their needs and feelings over his. In assessing what they had done to attempt to resolve the issue before coming to me, Lisa listed several things she had tried to change to make Tim feel less slighted. She talked about skipping a few family events thinking this would show him she wasn't spending all her time with them, and she had even stopped speaking with her parents every day, as had always been her habit.

When they returned to therapy Lisa felt happy with the changes she had made, which in her mind demonstrated to Tim that he was a priority and she was willing to sacrifice for him. When it was his turn to speak, however, Tim said he didn't feel anything had changed and offered several examples of "evidence" from the past few weeks. Lisa then became irate, reiterating that she had done "everything" while he had "obviously made no effort to recognize" the changes she'd made when really she wanted to change nothing.

The problem was, Lisa had made changes she thought Tim would agree reflected what he wanted. She made no effort to ask him what he was looking for or what he wanted, almost confirming his accusation that she didn't care about what he wanted or thought. Now, after hearing her talk about all she had done, he accused her of making only the changes that suited her. They both left the session feeling angry and invalidated. They didn't come back to therapy, reporting later that they had decided to separate. Lisa reiterated her opinion that she had made too many changes and had tried "everything," while he wasn't willing to change at all and would never be satisfied.

The takeaway here is to consult others when you are creating solutions to problems that involve them, rather than simply dictating those solutions. Be mindful of concluding that your actions are not the problem and if everyone else in your life would just do what you want and see things your way everything would be fine. You need to be willing to make a decision that you would rather be happy than right.

Rule #14

When Someone Makes a Change You Asked Them to Make, it Still Counts

Recall Rule #10, which addresses allowing yourself to be angry at someone for not doing what you want them to do *without identifying* what you do want them to do. Rule #14 involves telling someone exactly what you want and how you want them to do it, then getting mad at them because "You did that only because I asked you to." As you can see, this is a trap, a no-win situation for the other party.

I have found that this "solution" usually falls into one of two categories. First, you are angry at the other person because they "should just know" what you need and want without having to explain it to them (refer back to Rule #10). The anger associated with this familiar scenario is usually secondary to hurt, sadness, and disappointment.

When someone is passionate about someone or something, they tend to put a great deal of resources (energy, time, money, et cetera) into that particular thing. For example, if someone enjoys football they may figure out at the beginning of the week (or maybe even as early as the beginning of the season) what time the game is on and who their team is playing. They may call friends to come over to watch the game, plan out and shop for the foods and beverages they want, and make sure they have completed all the other necessary tasks ahead of time so nothing gets in the way of the big event. This is what it looks like when someone is passionate. It is very clear they find joy in the undertaking and don't see it as a burden. People light up when they engage in something they are passionate about, raising their vibrations and attracting others.

When two people show this level of passion for their relationship there is no greater feeling. The trick to maintaining a healthy relationship over time is to keep the fires of passion burning while simultaneously providing the security everyone craves. The problem is that it often becomes an either-or proposition, with partners trading the passion for the security. They begin to slack off on putting energy into maintaining the passion for the other person or the relationship, creating hurt and loneliness, to name a few lower-vibrational emotions.

Partners can feel the reduction of that passion and fire as it is redirected toward other things such as watching sports. They see that something else getting the attention and energy once put into them and it hurts. If we're talking about Rule #14, they let their partner know what they want, for example, that they should plan a weekend together and make sure nothing gets in the way, just like they manage to do with football Sunday. All you really want is to see that level of energy put into your relationship. You want to know your time together is something he/she would fight for.

You could also apply this to a relationship with a parent, sibling or other family member. For example, "Since you started your new job you don't make plans to come over for Sunday dinner anymore." Now, this statement is a bit less direct, but it gets the point across. Either way, the husband or the daughter or whoever does the thing the other person said they want, only to be met with anger. In my experience, that anger, expressed in the form of "it doesn't count because I asked you to do it," is secondary to "I'm hurt because you don't put your energy into me/our relationship that I see you putting into other things."

Note how this relates to Rule #2: "Don't 'should' all over others." This is when one feels as though no one meets your expectations so they feel justified in coming down on anyone who "should" know and disappoints them anyway. In the case of Rule #14, the disappointment also stems from the fact that they should have known, the only difference is that you made the attempt to tell them. For example, your partner is aware that you love flowers but they never get them. Then, after you happen to mention that you love flowers, they come home the next day with flowers, and the anger ensues. Clearly, you tell them, they only did it because you asked them to. My response to this is, "So what?!", but most people would rather focus on the fact that the other person had to be told, rather than focusing on the fact that they got what they asked for.

Consider this example that may sound familiar from your own childhood (and perhaps has also played out in your home). Your parents, after getting a call from your teachers that you haven't been doing your homework, bring you downstairs for a "talk." You agree to go to your room to do your homework but stomp up the stairs, letting everyone know you aren't happy about it. How many of you got into trouble for stomping up the stairs, instead of getting praised for going up to do your homework without yelling or crying?

The important takeaway here is for you to focus on someone giving you what you have asked for, rather than telling them it "doesn't count" because you "should do it without having to be asked." Trust me, if you don't validate someone making the effort, you greatly reduce their willingness to do it the next time. Yes, you may get across the message you are hurt that they didn't figure it out, but potentially at a great cost.

PART III

Regain Your Life

Chapter Six

THE MORE THINGS CHANGE, THE MORE THEY STAY THE SAME...

Now you have read through all "The Rules" and are aware of some of the distorted thinking patterns that sabotage your heartfelt attempts to resolve issues and get your needs met. Your work, however, is just beginning. As you process what you experienced as you went through them, you will begin to experience a shift in how you process daily interactions with others. You won't be able to engage with your world in the same way as you play out various situations and come to understand them from a higher vibration. As this occurs, it's important for you to remember that change can feel threatening, even though you are making improvements. People who you interact with may or may not appreciate and applaud your changes because they are reacting to the discomfort of the expectations change can bring. Even you may feel and rebuke the changes when you begin to experience the discomfort of moving from what was once comfortable.

Homeostasis, which is defined by Biologydictionary.net as "an organism's process of maintaining a stable internal environment suitable for sustaining life," is a term typically used in reference to systems in the body (i.e. lymphatic, cardiovascular, et cetera) and biology of living creatures.

The assumption of any system is that it will function in a way that promotes stability, and that any change in any part of the system will have a ripple effect on the rest of the system. For example, if a foreign germ enters your body and threatens disease, the systems of your body will react simultaneously to get rid of the invader to bring harmony and balance back to all systems. In this example, your body will divert all its sources of energy to create a hostile environment (fever) for the germ, leaving you exhausted.

Homeostasis can also apply to ecosystems as well. As a soul living in a human body, we are each part of a variety of systems that touch our everyday lives on a number of different levels. Unless you live completely alone you are considered a system with those you live with, including any animals. You are a part of a system within both your immediate and extended family. You are a part of a system with your friend group and at your job. Following the basic assumption of homeostasis, like any system one change in any part will result in a reaction to attempt to bring things back to balance. Within the system you interact with as an employee, if someone doesn't show up for work the other coworkers must work together to ensure the job still gets done. If someone in your family is having a bad day or isn't feeling well, the other members of the system will be impacted by the change in energy for the day. The other members of the system will somehow have to make up for what the ill member isn't doing so things will continue to run as smoothly as possible.

Note that a system does not always run in what everyone might consider to be a healthy manner. This is immaterial with regard to homeostasis, meaning the rest of the system will still react to bring its environment back to balance, even if that balance is dysfunctional. It is not unusual for clients to initially come into therapy because something happened that pushed their system into chaos.

I was working with a family that consisted of Sheila, Ted, and their three children. Sheila had been an alcoholic for years; in fact, Ted said she had been a problematic drinker since just after they married eleven years earlier, and the kids couldn't remember a time when their mother didn't have an alcohol addiction. It was part of their family system. My question was, why did they wait so long before coming for help?

In session, they recounted the story of the night Sheila drove home drunk from and "finally got caught." She totaled the family car (thankfully no one was seriously hurt) and she was court-mandated to counseling, both alone and with the family. Sheila was a functional alcoholic. She held down a full-time job and her drinking had not, up to this point, resulted in any issues at work. She never called in sick and was a good employee. She was in sales and it is the culture in sales to bring clients out for dinner and drinks to discuss business, so she didn't drink any more or less than those she interacted with as a part of her job. Typically, she was intoxicated by dinnertime after an afternoon of drinking with colleagues and clients, and it was not uncommon for her to return home after the children were already in bed. According to all three kids, Ted functioned as both mom and dad, helping them with homework, making meals, and taking them to their activities, with the help of his parents. The kids also agreed that their home life looked very differently from their friends', but it was "just how things were." They didn't know anything else.

Then the accident happened. Sheila was hospitalized and detoxed and went through a court process following her arrest. Things in this family's daily life changed. She was now home from work at dinnertime, and she was sober. She began to be a part of her children's lives by helping with homework and attending school functions and meetings with teachers. Ted was thrilled to have an equal partner help with the household responsibilities and was anxious to have his wife back. Initially, everyone was happy to have Sheila be a more active part of the system.

Over time, however, things began to break down. Now that Sheila was present, she and Ted frequently argued over disciplining the children and how the money was spent. The kids began testing the rules, seeing that their parents didn't agree about the rules of the home. The pieces of the system began to shift back to where things were "comfortable." Though everyone said they were thrilled that Sheila was sober, the family system was thrown into chaos and no one was happy. Eventually, absent the proper education and support, homeostasis fully kicked in. Sheila went back to drinking, her family resumed operating as they had before the accident, when everyone knew exactly what to expect each day. Despite its dysfunction, this family had come to find security in that routine and each member of the system, albeit unconsciously, played a role in its return.

Homeostasis is often the reason people struggle with solutions that result in more problems. As mentioned, they recognize that the way things are not healthy and need to change, yet at the same time they fear that change. It is easier for them to believe everything they are doing is correct and/or tell themselves it is others around them who have to make changes. It becomes too overwhelming to consider changing their own thoughts, emotions or behavioral patterns, particularly if they have been embedded for years and are traumatic.

Activity: The Biology of Change

Homeostasis must be taken into account as you attempt to change; in fact, it is one of the most important pieces you must evaluate and consider as you move through the process of creating a life that is more fulfilling. Take some time to reflect on what changes you may have to make to improve the overall quality of your life. Also reflect on how these changes may have an impact (negative, positive, or neutral) on those in your system or your system as a whole. Will anyone, including you, not be happy with the changes? What resistance do you imagine will come up when you think about making changes?

CUT THE SHIT

Chapter Seven

AND NOW A WORD FROM SPIRIT

When our loved ones pass to the spirit world, they learn new insights into what they experienced while in human form. They also attempt to communicate these learnings to us so we can improve our lives and hopefully not repeat their mistakes. Oftentimes the living are not aware of, or do not understand, these messages and turn to those with the gift of mediumship for help. Since discovering and embracing my mediumship, I have begun offering contacts with loved ones alongside my counseling practice as a tool for healing and accessing joy and comfort.

When Jade walked into my office, I immediately sensed the presence of her twin brother, Jackson. He allowed me to experience a sudden, painful sensation to my head, the result of the self-inflicted wound that ended his life. He admitted that he had been an angry and resentful person during his life, which he had come to understand stemmed from his feelings of hurt, sadness, and betrayal. These feelings had tormented him and eventually led to his decision to commit suicide. Jackson shared that Jade, too, was angry, resentful, and not living a life that served her highest good. He had come through to tell her that she should seek help to release her anger and talk about their shared abuse experiences so she could return to wholeness. As I delivered Jackson's message to her, Jade cried and admitted that she held onto a great deal of anger that kept her from experiencing the joy life has to offer.

Not every reading I do is by appointment, but sometimes in response to immediate need. One day, my old friend Michelle contacted me in a panic. Michelle was still trying to heal from the loss of her father the previous year when her husband suffered a brain bleed and was admitted to ICU. Now she was sitting by his bedside, contemplating another devastating loss and desperate to hear from Spirit that this would not happen. Sure enough, her father immediately stepped forward and communicated that the incident with her husband was a wake-up call to start focusing on his health. Michelle's father also wanted her to know he hadn't heeded those warnings himself, which had led to his untimely death. As soon as I said the words I could feel her dad's relief that his message had finally been delivered. He had been trying to share this information with Michelle directly but she wasn't picking up on it. Michelle also expressed her relief and her gratitude for the message. Her husband was later discharged from the ICU and returned home, hopefully to change his lifestyle.

Maria came for a reading just after Christmas. Several of her loved ones came through, however, the one person she wanted to hear from waited until the end to share her message. Maria's mother had passed away only a few months earlier, leaving Maria not only struggling to get into the holiday season but questioning their entire relationship. Maria had decided to seek guidance from a medium after she and her younger sister attended the reading of their mother's will. Maria was shocked and embarrassed to learn that her sister "got everything," while she was not even mentioned at all!

She also expressed a deep feeling of betrayal, saying, "I did everything for her and my sister did nothing. I spent my whole life trying to please her. Why didn't she leave me anything?"

Maria's mother expressed great remorse and told her something I hear in many families – that she saw her younger daughter as vulnerable, weak, and someone who needed extra support. Maria, on the other hand, had always seemed able to take care of herself without assistance from others. Her mother didn't worry about how she would survive and therefore left everything to the younger sister who "needed it."

Once someone passes away, they are able to see a reflection of interactions they had throughout their life, and the impact of their actions on others, in a way they couldn't during their human life. Maria's mother made me understand that at the time she made the will she lacked awareness of how Maria would feel at being excluded. She also wanted to make sure Maria knew just how much she appreciated and loved her. Furthermore, she validated Maria empathy for the feelings of others – something she had sometimes lacked during her life. The lesson she passed to Maria was that her actions and choices were a reflection of her own shortcomings, not a reflection of Maria. When others treat you poorly, it is often a reflection of their "stuff," not yours.

The "Rules" from this book have been intuitively provided to me for my own learning and development and also to be taught to you. Our loved ones want us to be able to learn these lessons with grace and ease so we can improve the quality of our relationships and daily lives. It is one of my greatest honors to be able to share the learnings and teachings from the spirit world as blessings to the word of the living. Keep in mind that we are all given the gift of being able to tap into the wisdom of the spiritual realm. Spirit frequently shares they are always around their loved ones and are eager to share the lessons they have learned, but they are not being acknowledged.

The most frequent message from loved ones in spirit are to live the life that is a blessing to you, not what you think others want from you. Most importantly, loved ones want you to know they have never left you. They are constantly around, just in a different form. They hear when you talk to them. They remind you that you will always make the right choice if it comes from a place of love, with love of yourself being on the top of the list. When you love and respect yourself, love will flow freely from and to you.

Chapter Eight

YOUR NEW LIVER

As I look back on the process of writing this book, I realize it was in my head, sorting itself out and waiting to be written, for most of my professional life. I think you will find many authors who will echo this sentiment. Successful authors are intuitively guided to share a message and when we listen to this guidance it becomes our life's work. I don't just mean it's something we do for a career, I mean we own it and it becomes a part of our DNA.

When I first sat down to write, I didn't truly understand how profound this project would become. If you go back and re-read Chapter 1, you will recall that I wasn't quite ready to tell my whole story. In the processing of writing, however, things changed dramatically, and now here I am sharing it with you as a part of my soul's purpose on this planet. You see, I've spent the past six weeks, not only writing about these lessons for you, but finishing them for myself.

As this book was nearing completion, my father died at the age of seventy-three. He had lived a difficult life and spent much of it hiding from his demons. After decades of drinking and eventual liver disease, four years ago he was given a second chance in the form of a transplant. Indeed, for a brief time following the surgery I thought I saw hope that he could be different. He could learn from his mistakes and take advantage of a second chance others would kill for and never get. This didn't happen, friends. My dad had an extra four years literally gifted to him and still he didn't learn these lessons. Because of how he lived and the choices he made I always knew he wouldn't live to be an elderly man and, cognitively, I thought I was prepared for it.

Despite the fact that he hurt me in so many ways over the years, I had always been the bigger person – sending Christmas cards, calling him every few weeks, and sending him a picture of my horses here and there... until that last year, when I recognized being around him was far too toxic and pulled back in order to protect myself. He never questioned it or even noticed, for that matter. He was so entrenched in his life and choices that he always came back to the same place.

Since his death I can tell you firsthand that you cannot prepare yourself for what you will deal with when your parent dies. Previously I had come to the understanding that he would never be the father I wanted or needed. I knew there would be no last-minute revelations and he would tell me how sorry he was. It would have been so healing to get at least one "I love you" or "I'm proud of you." It would have meant so much for him to just hug me. That never happened, and suddenly there I was watching the man who had literally terrorized me, my mother and my brother take his last breath, and take any small glimmer of hope that he would do any one of those things right along with him.

He left no will, no life insurance, no money to bury him, and a house stockpiled with fifty years of paperwork and junk for us to deal with. In going through all of what he left behind we have found more evidence of secrets and choices over the years that far surpass the lies and destruction we were aware of. Trust me, someday I will write a book about this process, but for now I will share all you need to know to make my point. I've been where you are. I've been abused in more ways than one. There is no fairytale ending to my story with my father. His death, however, marked the end of all the false narratives about who I thought I was – lies upon lies, and behind it all betrayal so enormous it would have been inconceivable had I not seen that "evidence" for myself.

This isn't the ending to MY story, though. This is an opportunity for me to learn and grow and pass my lessons on to you so you can have a happy ending.

It's your turn now. Your trauma and history of bad experiences and unsatisfying relationships do not have to define you. You have choices. There are no exceptions to this. YOU HAVE CHOICES. You don't think you do, but you do. Remember the lessons on homeostasis? Remember what I said about entitling yourself to make bad choices, acting as if you are better than others, and giving yourself permission to point the finger at others when you are not perfect yourself? Most importantly, remember the lesson that no matter what you have been through you never have permission to focus your energy on how others need to work harder than you at making you happy, all because you got screwed?

It is within these lessons, these Rules, that the magic resides.

Henry Ford said, "Whether you think you can or whether you think you can't, you're right." Henry knew the secret to managing energy. Whatever energy you decide to put into the Universe will be what you create. This is your "new liver," your chance to stop making choices that seal the fate you tell yourself will never change. These lessons were mine to learn so I could pass them along with both the wisdom and knowledge of how the Universe and energy work so you can find the life that blesses you NOW!

I know what you are thinking: "Becc, you don't understand what has happened to me." I may not understand exactly what you have experienced. No one can. Your story and experiences are uniquely yours and no one can ever tell you they know what you are feeling. By now you get the message. If you have gotten this far in my process, you have come to understand you, and you alone are the only one who is responsible for changing your circumstances. YOU.

I am not trying to minimize what you have been through. I'm not going to argue that you don't have every right to feel all the anger, resentment, loneliness, desperation, fear, terror, abandonment, betrayal, worry, anxiety, embarrassment, hopelessness and whatever else you experience. You absolutely have that right and that choice. Yup, I said it. It's a choice.

This reminds me of a story I've shared with many of my clients. Like most people, I absolutely hate going to the dentist. In fact, as a kid I made a decision that once I turned eighteen I would never go again – no one could make me. Eventually, though, I got over it and made an appointment for a cleaning. I saw a sign that day in the office that said, "You don't have to floss all your teeth, just the ones you want to keep." This hit me. You don't have to do anything you don't want to do, but just know your decisions have consequences. Choosing to make others responsible for making changes, and telling yourself you are right in doing so, is only mimicking the patterns that hurt you in the first place. Repeating patterns of poor choices, not taking responsibility for your choices, and giving others the power to control your energy resources leaves you stuck in a cycle of unsatisfying relationships.

The quote from Haruki Murakami bears repeating: "Pain is inevitable, suffering is optional." Follow the wisdom and knowledge I have outlined in "The Rules" to raise your vibrations and bring blessings and abundance into your life. The choice is yours, so choose wisely and, when you are tempted to return to your own "homeostasis," remember all that you read in this book, that you have been called out to "Cut the Shit."

About the Author

Rebecca (Becc) Nelson has been in the business of assisting people in their pursuit of transformation since 1992. Becc's work focuses on those who are inspired to move to the next level of their lives but find themselves repeating patterns of behavior that no longer serve them, keeping them stuck and feeling frustrated. Becc has a master's degree in Marriage and Family Therapy and is a licensed chemical dependency professional and marriage and family therapist. She is also an ordained minister. She has worked in a variety of levels of treatment in the mental health and substance abuse fields, as well as spiritual coaching. Though her clients range from children to older adults, her special passion lies in helping individuals and couples function at their highest level, in their relationship and as co-parents.

In 2010, Becc and her husband Ed opened their own healing and transformational business, Hope Counseling and Mediation Center, INC, where they offer individual and couple's therapy, divorce mediation, and spiritual coaching. Becc uses an approach to therapy and transformation she calls the "Loving Authority," combining systemic approaches to identifying and solving dysfunctional patterns. This approach allows Becc to assertively approach transformation with the direct energy needed to inspire both motivation and changes in attitudes and behavior her clients want and need but have become too overwhelmed and exhausted to manage alone.

Becc is available for spiritual coaching for individuals and couples, psychic and mediumistic readings, various metaphysical/spiritual classes, and angel readings. She also is available for speaking engagements and performing weddings and celebrations of life.

Becc currently lives on her historic farm property in Rhode Island with her husband, Ed.

Continue the Journey with Medium and Healer, Becc Nelson, LMFT

Thank you for choosing to read my book and allow me to be a part of your transformational journey. The greatest gift we can give ourselves is to challenge our current beliefs and ideas and encourage growth. If you would like to continue working with me personally, please visit one or both of the links below and check out the options for more intensive healing work with a personalized treatment plan specific to your goals and transformational journey.

Becc Nelson's Services | Spiritual Counseling
Lincoln, RI

www.beccnelson.com

Becc Nelson, LMFT Intuitive & Spiritual Coach
Live Stream - YouTube

www.youtube.com/watch?v=KPVjo-8fryo

On my site you can also download a free bonus gift, *The Reveal Journal,* which is a companion to this book:

www.beccnelson.com/cts-book-gift

Acknowledgments

To my mother, Kathy, thank you for always loving me without conditions. You always believed in me, even when I didn't believe in myself. You were always my biggest fan and I owe my tenacity and bravery to you. You are a true survivor who also taught me the power of "self" and faith.

To my husband Ed, you have been by my side for better or for worse for over thirty years. You have been there to support every idea I have and always cheered me on. No matter the cost or risk you always made things happen when you could see I was passionate about something, including this book. I am grateful for your undying support and love and all the times you took on the other tasks so I could get it out into the world.

To my daughter, Taylor, who truly teaches me unconditional love every day. No matter how grown you are, you still look at me as if I'm the most powerful and magical person in the world. Everyone should have a daughter who loves and believes in their mother like you do, and I am grateful for you every day of my life.

To my father, Harry, who passed away as I was writing this book. You have taught me to be the healer I am and I feel you guiding my journey in spirit. I am grateful for you and the lessons your life taught me.

To my friend and psychic medium, Debbie Squizzero. I knew I had to meet you after you told a mutual friend that you saw a "special supportive person" over her shoulder. That was over ten years ago, and I continue to cherish our friendship and be inspired by your path and choices. I also credit the very honest and loving advice you gave me nearly two years ago with kicking off my spiritual journey, and for this I will be forever grateful.

To Michelle Barr, my first mentor who has spent countless hours in calls, classes, and texting conversations to support and guide me on my journey and help give my book the energy it needed to become real. Thank you for this, and for taking the time to write a beautiful reflection of its essence that I am proud to share. I am grateful for you.

To Lindsay Marino, who continues to support and guide my journey as a medium. More than once I have come to you with doubt and confusion and you lovingly remind me who I really am and what I am capable of. I am grateful for you.

To Sunny Dawn Johnston, who has been a loving guide to and for me, particularly over my journey within the past year as I transition into a full-time healer, doing the work of Spirit. Your loving and down-to-earth guidance always grounds me and reminds me to stay focused and on task in a way that leaves me fired up and ready to move. I am particularly grateful for your assistance through some very difficult personal work I did over the past year, which has allowed me to learn the necessary lessons and move to a more powerful level of my true soul journey as a healer and teacher. I am grateful for you.

Finally, to Shanda Trofe, who has been more than patient and supportive in my writing journey. You gave more than was required and spent literally countless hours reading, reviewing, coaching and cheerleading my journey. You helped me to believe this book was possible, even when I was ready to give up. I am grateful for you.

Made in United States
North Haven, CT
14 October 2022